W9-BUW-324

ASIAN ART & CULTURE

Published by the ARTHUR M. SACKLER GALLERY,

Smithsonian Institution, Washington, D.C.,

THE SILK ROAD PROJECT, INC., and the

UNIVERSITY OF WASHINGTON PRESS, Seattle and London

Along the SILK ROAD

ELIZABETH TEN GROTENHUIS, EDITOR

Copyright © 2002 Smithsonian Institution
All rights reserved.
Published as part of the Asian Art & Culture
series by the Arthur M. Sackler Gallery,
Smithsonian Institution, Washington, D.C.
in association with the University of
Washington Press, Seattle and London,
and the Silk Road Project, Inc.

The publication of this book is supported in
part by the Silk Road Project, Inc. and by the
Donald E. Ellegood International
Publications Endowment

Asian Art & Culture series editor:
Karen Sagstetter
Designer: Carol Beehler
Typeset in Adobe Garamond by General
Typographers, Inc., Washington, D.C.
Printed in Hong Kong

Cover: Detail, Kenro Izu, *Lamayuru
Monastery, Ladakh,* 1999. See fig. 5.6.

Back cover: Kenro Izu, *Chuku Monastery,
Tibet,* 2000. See fig. 5.1.

Title page: Detail, Kenro Izu, *Bezeklik Caves,
Turfan, China,* 2000. See fig. 5.10.

Frontispiece: Detail, *Majnun Approaches the
Camp of Layli's Caravan* from a manuscript of
the *Haft Awrang* of Jami, Iran, 1556–65.
Opaque watercolor, gold, and silver on paper,
folio 253a, 23.5 x 19.5 cm. Freer Gallery of Art,
Smithsonian Institution, Washington, D.C.,
purchase, F1946.12. Although this detail of a
sixteenth-century Persian painting dates later
than the heyday of the historical Silk Road, it
gives, nonetheless, a sense of what activities
within an encampment might have looked
like on a caravan route in West Asia.

Copyright page, top to bottom:
Detail, face at Angkor Thom, Cambodia.
See p. 86.
Detail, Plate, Iran. See fig. 4, p. 19.
Detail, *Courtly Entertainment,* Bukhara,
present-day Uzbekistan. See p. 14.
Detail, Pair of Painted Pottery Female
Dancers, China. See p. 56.

Maps: pages 12–13, 20, 41, and 108 by Gene
Thorpe

Library of Congress
Cataloging-in-Publication Data

Along the Silk Road /
Elizabeth ten Grotenhuis, editor.
p. cm. — (Asian art & culture; no. 6)
Published to accompany the
Silk Road Project, Inc.
Includes bibliographical references and index.
ISBN 0-295-98182-2
1. Asia — Civilization. 2. Silk Road — Songs
and music. I. Ten Grotenhuis, Elizabeth.
II. Silk Road Project, Inc. III. Asian art &
culture (numbered); vol. 6.
DS12.A49 2001   2001-040730
950 — dc21   CIP

The paper used in this publication meets the
minimum requirements for the American
National Standard for Permanence of Paper
for Printed Library Materials, z39.48-1984.

Board of the Freer Gallery of Art and
the Arthur M. Sackler Gallery

Mrs. Nancy Fessenden, chair
Mr. Richard M. Danziger, vice chair
Dr. Siddharth K. Bhansali
Mrs. Mary Ebrahimi
Mr. George Fan
Dr. Robert Feinberg
Dr. Kurt Gitter
*Katharine Graham in memoriam
Mrs. Richard Helms
Sir Joseph E. Hotung
Mrs. Ann Kinney
Mr. H. Christopher Luce
Mrs. Jill Hornor Ma
Mr. Paul Marks
Ms. Elizabeth Meyer
Mrs. Daniel P. Moynihan
Mr. Frank H. Pearl
Dr. Martin Powers
Dr. Gursharan Sidhu
Mr. Michael Sonnenreich
Mr. Abolala Soudavar
Prof. Elizabeth ten Grotenhuis
Mr. Paul F. Walter
Ms. Shelby White

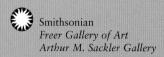

Smithsonian
*Freer Gallery of Art
Arthur M. Sackler Gallery*

CONTENTS

MILO CLEVELAND BEACH

Former Director, Freer Gallery of Art and Arthur M. Sackler Gallery
Smithsonian Institution

The world's attention was captured recently by the horrific destruction of the monumental Buddhist sculptures at Bamiyan, an act dramatically documented by CNN. The site was carved into the side of a steep range of hills in western Afghanistan and one of the figures, fifty-three meters (175 feet) high, had been the largest Buddhist image in existence. These figures, constructed perhaps circa 600 C.E., were intended to be seen from great distances; one of their purposes, clearly, was to attract travelers passing through the valley. Bamiyan was among the many sites that provided accommodations where travelers of the time could stay and where supplies were available. Often built and supported by religious communities, the sites also provided opportunities for missionary teaching about religious beliefs. Another purpose of Bamiyan, therefore, was to promote the ideals of wisdom and compassion basic to Buddhism.

The Bamiyan Valley, broad and flat, is interlaced with paths that have been used for millennia by merchants, monks, and adventurers. These routes were part of the greater Silk Road, the loose network of trails that crossed the mountains and deserts of Central Asia to connect East Asia and the Mediterranean. In its heyday, this was one of the most cosmopolitan areas on earth: merchants carrying fine silk and ornamented lacquers westward from China would mingle with traders bringing fragile Roman glass to the east, or with Indians seeking markets for superbly carved ivory cosmetic boxes or gold ornaments for fashionable women. (We know this because many such objects have been excavated in Afghanistan and were kept in the Kabul Museum until the tragic recent destruction of both the building and its collections.) It was by this route, too, that monks traveling north from India first brought Buddhism to East Asia. The Silk Road subsequently provided a means for converts in China, Korea, and Japan to visit India to investigate the source of their new beliefs.

Along the way, caravansaries and small settlements marked stages of the journey. Bamiyan was one of these, albeit a particularly elaborate example. The hills behind the Bamiyan images were carved into rooms—monks' cells and shrines. When travelers arrived, they were sometimes asked to pay for their stay by helping with the construction, maintenance, or (if their skills were such) decoration of the buildings. Silk Road sites often show an intermingling of architectural or artistic styles that can be traced to the homelands of these travelers: China, the varying regions of Central Asia, India, and

Iran, as well as the Roman world, among other regions. At these sites, travelers were continually introduced to new and unfamiliar artistic and architectural styles and techniques, new lifestyles, and

Buddhas at monastic site, Bamiyan, Afghanistan
Photograph by Richard Edwards, 1968

different religious traditions. And the buildings, decorations, and objects that remained have documented the early stages of these international cultural contacts and cross-influences, interactions that continue today in the remarkable Silk Road Project celebrated in this volume.

That anything from such an ancient period has survived is virtually miraculous. Many of the sites, especially those built of wood or other fragile materials, have simply disintegrated in the harsh climatic conditions of Central Asia. Others were literally buried under the drifting sands of the region's desert landscapes. The recent actions of the ruling Taliban in Afghanistan have demonstrated another threat to the fragility of these remains, however. This is the willful destruction that one group, acting alone, can incur, and the historical and aesthetic loss to all of humanity that can result. The Bamiyan images had been attacked many times in the past: in the thirteenth century by the armies of Genghis Khan and in the seventeenth century by troops of the Mughal emperor Aurangzeb, for example, but never more than casually. The complete destruction of the images and of related sites and objects throughout Afghanistan is an act of unrivaled cultural brutality. But it also reveals a tragic situation in purely human terms,

Buddha at monastic site, Bamiyan,
Afghanistan
Photograph by Richard Edwards, 1968

for the ruin of those material objects was preceded by the destruction of human and cultural value systems, which led to these acts of rage.

As political empires shifted, and travelers used other routes, the Silk Road regions of Central Asia became increasingly isolated—physically, economically, and culturally. In their own defense, the Taliban have articulated this status movingly. Why, they asked, was the world so willing to protest the threatened destruction of ancient images from a religion no longer of importance in the region, but so indifferent to the living Afghan people, who were then (and remain) overwhelmingly homeless and facing starvation? And, as if to prove the point, once the images had been destroyed, the media again ignored Afghanistan. The area had been a thriving cosmopolitan center during the centuries when the Silk Road was a prime route of communication, but its growing isolation allowed the varying peoples of Afghanistan to forget the significant place they hold in the history of human interactions on this planet.

Now, when the time comes for Afghanistan to emerge from its troubles and reconstruct itself, cultural artifacts and sites that should revive pride and create identity will no longer be there. That may be the greatest tragedy of all.

The Freer Gallery of Art and the Arthur M. Sackler Gallery, which together form the national museum of Asian art for the United States of America, and the Silk Road Project, Inc., an international program of cultural activities, have joined to produce this volume of Asian Art & Culture in honor of the multiyear events sponsored by the project. The cultural programs sponsored by the galleries, and by the Silk Road Project at partner cities throughout Asia, Europe, and North America, seek to increase awareness among both participants and audiences of the variety and richness of unfamiliar traditions and the importance of understanding viewpoints different from one's own. The cellist Yo-Yo Ma, who initiated the Silk Road Project, has remarked that the Internet is in some ways a contemporary equivalent to the communication channels of the ancient Silk Road. With the great developments in communication promised for the twenty-first century, we must all of us ensure that no peoples on this planet are involuntarily isolated either from other peoples or from awareness of and pride in their own cultural identities. •

This volume owes a great deal to many people. Milo Cleveland Beach, former director of the Freer Gallery of Art and Arthur M. Sackler Gallery, first suggested the idea and has been a supporter through all stages of preparation. Karen Sagstetter, head of publications at the Freer and Sackler galleries and editor par excellence, worked with all the authors, paying attention to every detail of writing and illustration, while Carol Beehler provided inspired vision as art director. Thanks to Vidya Dehejia, deputy director and chief curator, and to the curators and staff at the Freer and Sackler galleries who gave unstintingly of their time and energy. Special thanks to Stephen Allee, museum research specialist in Chinese; Louise Cort, curator for ceramics; Debra Diamond, assistant curator of South and Southeast Asian art; Massumeh Farhad, associate curator of Islamic art; Ann C. Gunter, associate curator of ancient Near Eastern Art; Jan Stuart, associate curator of Chinese art; James Ulak, curator of Japanese art; Colleen Hennessey, archivist; and David Hogge, slide librarian. Editor Ann Hofstra Grogg and indexer Michelle Smith provided editorial expertise, while designer Patricia Inglis perfected the layout.

We are grateful for partial support toward production of this volume by the Silk Road Project, Inc. We thank the staff in the Silk Road Project office in New York, who helped with many details—Jean Davidson, Rachel Derkits, Makiko Freeman, and Esther Won. Thanks go to Cristin Bagnall and Brooke Thompson-Mills in the office of Yo-Yo Ma and to Jill Hornor, Sylvan Barnet, and William Burto, who were outside readers for three of the chapters. Pat Soden, director of the University of Washington Press, and the able production staff there helped bring the volume to bookstores around the world. •

TERMS USED IN THIS BOOK

B.C.E. AND C.E. Following a growing trend toward neutral terminology, we use in this book the designation B.C.E. (Before the Common Era) instead of B.C., and the designation C.E. (Common Era) instead of A.D.

WEST, CENTRAL, SOUTH, AND EAST ASIA Following the practice of the Freer and Sackler galleries, we have assigned certain terms to refer to areas of the broad landmass that stretches from the Mediterranean to the Pacific Ocean. *West Asia* identifies the countries (often called the Middle East) that lie closest to the Mediterranean. This general designation includes Iran. *Central Asia* refers to the contemporary Central Asian republics but may also refer in the essays that emphasize the historical Silk Road to the lands around the Tarim Basin, now the westernmost region of China. *South Asia* refers to India and *Southeast Asia* to countries in the southeastern corner of the landmass. *East Asia* refers to China, Korea, and Japan.

PERSIA AND IRAN In much of Western literature, the terms *Persia* and *Iran* have been used interchangeably to refer to a vast geographic area that extends from India to the Mediterranean. Strictly speaking, however, these two designations refer to quite different geographic, political, and cultural entities. *Persia* is derived from the word *Pars,* or *Persis,* as it was known to the ancient Greeks, and has a narrow and specific connotation—a mountainous region northeast of the Persian Gulf, where the city of Shiraz and the Achaemenid capital, Persepolis, are situated. The etymology of the word *Iran* is *Aryan* and refers to the Indo-European people and language that spread throughout this region. Connoting a much larger geographic-cultural domain, the term *Iran* has been in use since the Achaemenid period (ca. 550–331 B.C.E.). Although the use of *Persia* as the designation for the country is less current, it is still used in its adjectival form, that is, *Persian,* to mean language and culture.

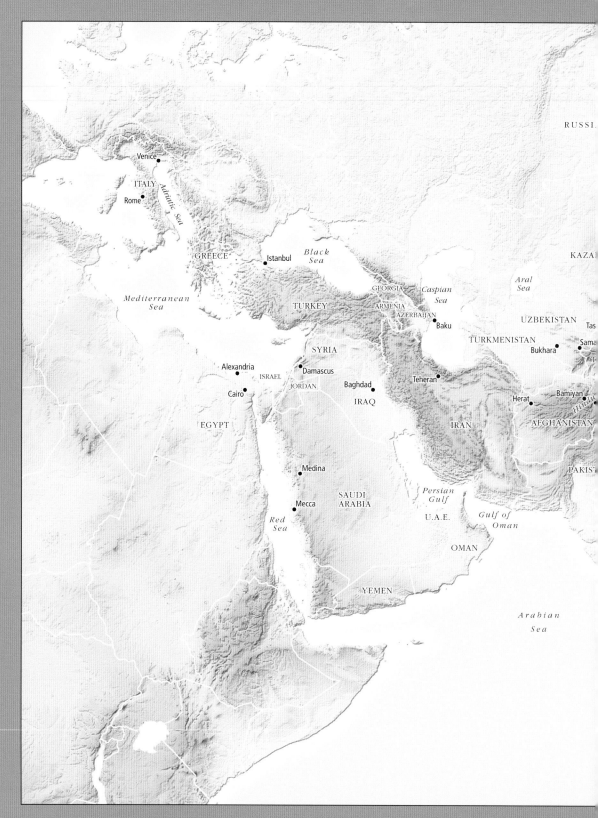

SILK ROAD LANDS

The Silk Road refers to trade routes that extended from Japan and China in East Asia across Central Asia, south to India, and west across the Iranian plateau and other lands to the Mediterranean. This historical network was at its height from about the second century B.C.E., when a Chinese envoy traveled into Central Asia, until the fourteenth century, when the Mongols safeguarded a northern land route that crossed the Eurasian steppes.

INTRODUCTION
THE SILK ROAD, ANCIENT AND CONTEMPORARY ELIZABETH TEN GROTENHUIS

Merchants traded many commodities along these routes—horses, jade, gems, glass, lacquer ware, spices, incense, tea, ivory, cotton, woolens, linens—but the term "Silk Road" (coined by the nineteenth-century German explorer Baron Ferdinand von Richthofen) evokes the material—silk—that the West especially craved.

Sericulture was well established in China by the second millennium B.C.E. Members of Chinese families, especially the women, became adept at cultivating mulberry trees and feeding the tender leaves to silkworms. They would watch carefully as the silkworms spun cocoons of silk fiber, dropping the cocoons into boiling

Courtly Entertainment in a manuscript of the *Haft manzar* (Seven Visages) by Hatifi; copied by Mir Ali. Painting attributed to Shaykhzada Musavvir, present-day Uzbekistan, Bukhara, 1538. Opaque watercolor, ink, and gold on paper; 25.9cm x 16.2cm. Freer Gallery of Art, Smithsonian Institution, purchase, F1956.14, folio 78. In the sixteeenth century, Bukhara, one of Central Asia's fabled Silk Road cities, became known for its vibrant cultural and artistic life.

2 Amphora, or two-handled jar with a narrow neck. China, Tang dynasty, 7th century. White stoneware with colorless glaze, 52.9 x 28.6 cm. Freer Gallery of Art, Smithsonian Institution, Washington, D.C., purchase, F1943.4. Such jars were first used by the ancient Greeks and Romans to transport oil or wine. A testament to the international-ism of the Tang dynasty, this glazed stoneware vessel was made in China, but it was based on a two-handled jar form introduced from the Mediterranean.

3 *The Abduction by Sea*, from a manuscript of the *Hasht Bihisht* (Eight Paradises), in the *Khamsa* (Quintet) by Amir Khusraw Dihlavi. Present-day Afghanistan, Herat, late 15th century. Opaque watercolor, gold, and silver on paper, 27 x 19.3 cm. Freer Gallery of Art, Smithsonian Institution, Washington, D.C., purchase, F1937.27. This painting presents a seascape in which the mounted figure on the near shore is wearing a crown that may have been inspired by a Mongol prototype.

water before the silkworms could break the silk filaments by bursting out of the cocoons in their transformation to moths. The boiling water softened the sticky protein called *sericin* that held the fibers together. These fibers were then unwound into continuous filaments that could extend from six hundred to a thousand meters. Because for many periods in China's history silk was used to pay taxes, skill at sericulture was an extremely important family activity.

The Greeks and Romans were uncertain how silk was made. Around 70 C.E. the Roman naturalist Pliny the Elder wrote that silk was a pale floss growing on leaves. The Roman Empire paid dearly for silk in gold and silver; Pliny estimated a hundred million sesterces a year, a staggering amount. In the first century B.C.E., silk was such a precious and rare commodity that even wealthy Romans could only afford small pieces, which they seem to have sewn like jeweled brooches onto their linen or woolen clothing. The amount of silk available began to increase in the first century C.E. when sea routes between China and the West were opened, complementing the overland routes. Remarkably, the production of silk remained a closely guarded secret and a Chinese monopoly for more than two thousand years, from the mid-second millennium B.C.E. to about the sixth century C.E., when the eggs of silkworms and the seeds of mulberry trees were smuggled to Byzantium and the process of sericulture was revealed to the West.

Silk Road lands were being shaped forty million years ago when what is now India collided with Eurasia. Intermediate periods of glaciation and warming followed, affecting the geography in important ways. We now understand that human beings had crossed and populated the vast Silk Road area sixty thousand or even seventy thousand years ago, well before the end of the last Ice Age, about ten thousand years ago. Agriculture, cities, science, and technology developed as early as eight thousand years ago. By 500 B.C.E. and for the next two thousand years, the Eurasian landmass linked four major centers of civilization: China, India, West Asia,

ونحوی کشتی رفت   پنج رضوان ل[ی]ک بشتی نم

شاه ارن سود نا[ک]   سرون ا[ر]د جوا[د]

and Europe. The Silk Road served as the major conduit for the transportation of knowledge and material goods between Asia and Europe during these two thousand years. It is also probably fair to say that until about 1500 C.E., or the beginning of the early modern period, Europe was something of a backwater compared to China, India, and West Asia.

All authors of this volume allude to or pay homage to the historical Silk Road. Some, however, emphasize a metaphoric use of the term to suggest cross-cultural exchange stretching much further back in time and, even more exciting, up to our own day. In the first chapter, cellist Yo-Yo Ma, who has called the Silk Road "the Internet of antiquity," introduces us to the metaphoric use of the term. In 1998 Ma founded the Silk Road Project, Inc., a nonprofit foundation devoted to the living arts of peoples of traditional Silk Road lands. One of the major components of this project has been the commissioning of new works by composers from Silk Road lands to be played in concerts and festivals throughout the world. This volume itself constitutes a part of the Silk Road Project activities, produced in collaboration with the Arthur M. Sackler Gallery, Smithsonian Institution, and the University of Washington Press. In conversation with ethnomusicologist Theodore Levin, the executive director of the Silk Road Project, Ma explores such questions as, "Does music still have an East and a West?" He discusses his sources of inspiration and authentic convergences in music.

The best-known segment of the historical Silk Road began in the Chinese capital of Chang'an, present-day Xi'an. Composer Bright Sheng spent two months, during the summer of 2000, following China's Silk Road from Xi'an to Kashgar. He closely followed the route of Zhang Qian, the second-century B.C.E. Chinese envoy who first traveled into the lands west of traditional China. Bright Sheng's findings are informative, exciting, and sometimes surprising. His insights about the integration of musical cultures along the modern-day Silk Road, illustrated with photographs taken on the journey, provide the basis for Chapter 2.

After leaving Chang'an/Xi'an and journeying west past Dunhuang (called Shazhou in earlier times) with its Thousand Buddha Caves, the Silk Road diverged into northern and southern routes that skirted the Central Asian Tarim Basin. The dreaded Taklamakan Desert, one thousand kilometers east to west and four hundred kilometers north to south, forms the major part of this basin. Local people warned that anyone who strayed by mistake into this huge wasteland, where dunes reach heights of ninety meters or more, would emerge a skeleton. But wonderful oasis towns with sophisticated cultures dotted the northern and southern routes encircling the desert. These oases, such as Turfan and Kucha on the northern route and Yarkand and Khotan on the southern route, provided havens for the camel caravans making the journey in relays from China

4 Plate. Iran, Sasanian dynasty, ca. 500–650 C.E.. Silver and gilt, diameter: 21.9 cm. Freer Gallery of Art, Smithsonian Institution, Washington, D.C., purchase, F1964.10. This impressive metal object's complex decoration testifies to cross-cultural exchange: In the center, the Greek god Dionysos (depicted here with female-like breasts) sits next to the princess Ariadne; to the right stands the hero Herakles. The plate depicts the god's triumphal arrival in India. A popular subject of Roman imperial art, it was later depicted over a wide area of the Byzantine Empire in textiles, gemstones, and metalwork, and transferred through such portable media to neighboring Sasanian Iran.

to the Mediterranean. The northern and southern routes encircling the Taklamakan Desert then converged at Kashgar to cross the Pamirs, one subsequent route headed for the great trading centers of Samarkand and Bukhara before crossing the Iranian plateau on the way to the Mediterranean cities of Antioch, Tyre, Aleppo, and Sidon. Other routes headed south from Yarkand and Khotan to India over the high Pamirs and from the sixth century across the Hindu Kush. Vital periods for the Silk Road were the Chinese Han dynasty (206 B.C.E.–220 C.E.), the Chinese Tang dynasty (618–907), and the Mongol khanate (thirteenth and fourteenth centuries, the age of Marco Polo). The Mongols, who ruled a vast empire, safeguarded a northern Silk Road land route that crossed the Eurasian steppes.

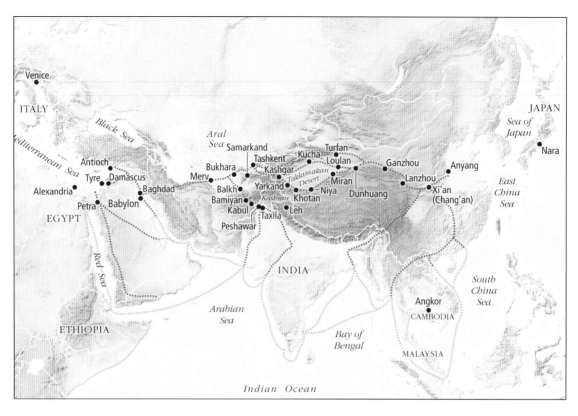

5 Silk Road Land and Sea Routes

It is important to emphasize, however, that until the Mongol period, hardly anyone made a round trip on the Silk Road or even a complete one-way trip. The routes
from China to the Mediterranean, over eight thousand kilometers long, passed through
many lands that were fiercely guarded for both political and mercantile reasons. One
camel caravan gave way to another, and the price of goods increased exponentially as
local taxes were levied and the number of middlemen increased. We know of no person
who journeyed the length of the Silk Road and back during Roman and Han dynasty
times and very few people who made round-trip journeys during the time when
Muslims ruled in West Asia and the Tang dynasty presided over a cosmopolitan culture
in China. Only during the late thirteenth and early fourteenth centuries, when the
Polos traveled from Venice to China and back, was east-west travel relatively safe.

In Chapter 3, archaeologist Elizabeth Barber explores the history of some of the
cloth, clothing, and rituals that crossed the Silk Road and survive to this day among
people living in Silk Road lands. Woolen textiles had been traveling east and west for
some two thousand years before silk was actively traded on the Silk Road. New fashions
in clothing spread, too, affecting sleeves and trousers as well as hats and ritual garments.
Fortunately, the dry desert sands of Central Asia have preserved some of these textiles—
woolen clothing and colorful fragments of silk.

Many other expressions of culture migrated the Silk Road. Buddhism, originating in India, but in eclipse there by the twelfth century, endures as a world religion because it traveled via the Silk Road north and east to Central Asia and East Asia, and via sea routes to parts of East Asia as well as to Southeast Asia. From the seventh century onward, Islam spread east and west from Arabia, the land of its origin. Other religions also flourished on the Silk Road—Zoroastrianism, Judaism, Nestorian Christianity, Manichaeism, Confucianism, Daoism, shamanism. In Chapter 4, art historian Elizabeth ten Grotenhuis uses a thirteenth-century Japanese Star Mandala, image of a Buddhist realm of enlightenment, as a springboard for discussing astrology and astronomy (the two were inseparable) along the Silk Road. Astrology, which for the ancients was intimately related to religion, was elaborately developed by the Babylonians by the middle of the first millennium B.C.E. Astrological concepts—including the signs of the zodiac—spread west to the Mediterranean and east to China from about this time. Ten Grotenhuis also links the Japanese Star Mandala to the ground plan of the early-thirteenth-century Cambodian city of Angkor Thom, which may be based on an Indian myth elaborated by Khmer astronomical ideas.

In Chapter 5, photographer Kenro Izu, known for his powerful platinum prints of world monuments, takes us to sacred sites along the Silk Road in India, Tibet, and China, destinations still vital to today's pilgrims. Art historian Debra Diamond vividly contextualizes these photographs. A number of Izu's photographs focus on one of the most important of Buddhist monuments—the stupa, or reliquary mound, perhaps better known in its East Asian form as the pagoda. After his death, the historical Buddha's body was cremated and his ashes divided. Stupas were raised over these ashes, as was the custom for royal burials and the burials of enlightened sages. The stupa/ pagoda functions as a funerary monument and a symbol of the Buddha's final enlightenment and release from this world.

Sea routes, important for trade and for communication, may also be considered part of the Silk Road, broadly interpreted. During the Han dynasty, Chinese ships traded with Southeast Asian kingdoms, and Indian and Malayan merchants traveled to South China. From the second century B.C.E., Greeks and Romans sailed from Red Sea ports to India, opening what is often called the Spice Route, while Arabs and Iranians sailed down the Persian Gulf to India and beyond. During the seventh and eighth centuries, Chinese, Korean, and Japanese ships crossing the East China Sea and the Sea of Japan brought continental goods to Japan. The eighth-century Shosoin collection of objects, which originally belonged to a Japanese emperor, is one of the most important group of Silk Road–related luxury items still in existence (see figs. 1.4, 1.5). Chinese ships also sailed to India and Iran and even, in the fifteenth century, to Africa. Indians

SILK ROAD TIMELINE

	BCE/CE	ACTUAL TIME	RELATED TO ONE YEAR
India hits Asia	40 MBCE	40 million years ago	1 year ago
Hominids walk upright in Asia	2.5 MBCE	2.5 million years ago	3 weeks ago
Homo sapiens sapiens appears	98 KBCE	100,000 years ago	21 hrs. ago
Last Ice Age glaciers retreat	8000 BCE	10,000 years ago	2 hrs. 8 min. ago
The Great Flood?	5500 BCE	7,500 years ago	1 hr. 36 min. ago
Neolithic societies occupy Eurasia	4000 BCE	6,000 years ago	1 hr. 18 min. ago
Indo-Europeans spread eastward and westward	4000 BCE	6,000 years ago	1 hr. 18 min. ago
Sphinx is built	3000 BCE	5,000 years ago	1 hr. 4 min. ago
Copper is smelted in West Asia	3000 BCE	5,000 years ago	1 hr. 4 min. ago
Bronze casting is practiced extensively in China	2000 BCE	4,000 years ago	51 min. ago
Ur and other Bronze Age city states fall	2000 BCE	4,000 years ago	51 min. ago
Sericulture begins in China	2000 BCE	4,000 years ago	51 min. ago
Oldest known glass in Egypt	2000 BCE	4,000 years ago	51 min. ago
Iron smelting is widely practiced in West Asia	1000 BCE	3,000 years ago	38 min. ago
Cast iron is known in China	400 BCE	2,400 years ago	30 min. ago
Alexander the Great burns Persepolis	331 BCE	2,331 years ago	30 min. ago
Zhang Qian travels	138 BCE	2,138 years ago	27 min. ago
Historic Silk Road era begins	100 BCE	2,100 years ago	27 min. ago
Common Era begins	0 CE	2,000 years ago	26 min. ago
Buddhism spreads out of India	100 CE	1,900 years ago	24 min. ago
Roman Empire falls	500 CE	1,500 years ago	19 min. ago
Chinese monopoly on silk ends	600	1,400 years ago	18 min. ago
Islam begins to spread	700	1,300 years ago	17 min. ago
Gunpowder is known in China	900	1,100 years ago	14 min. ago
Movable-type printing is used in China	1045	955 years ago	12 min. ago
Genghis Khan dies	1227	773 years ago	10 min. ago
Marco Polo goes to China	1271	729 years ago	9 min. ago
Cast iron arrives in Rhine Valley	1380	620 years ago	8 min. ago
Gutenberg's printing press developed	1458	542 years ago	7 min. ago
Historic Silk Road period ends	1500	500 years ago	6 min. ago
Internet becomes widespread	1995	5 years ago	4 sec. ago

and Arabs continued to trade along the southern sea routes, and in the sixteenth century Portuguese and other Europeans sailed to Asia.

Technologies and crafts also traveled the Silk Road. Metal smelting almost certainly began in West Asia and moved eastward, while other advances, notably in making cast iron and producing steel, moved from east to west. Glass manufacturing (see Chapter 3) began in West Asia and the Mediterranean and spread to East Asia by the middle of the first millennium B.C.E.; imported glass beads were often valued like gems. Gunpowder was known in China by the ninth century C.E. but did not reach the West for another five hundred years. In Chapter 6, materials scientist Merton C. Flemings traces transfers of technologies along the Silk Road up to the present day. He reminds us how modern travel and communications, and now, perhaps most important of all, the Internet, enable linkages akin to those enjoyed by people in premodern times who traveled the physical Silk Road. He also introduces us to the concept of "distance education."

Film historian Hamid Naficy in Chapter 7 presents an overview of groundbreaking Iranian films such as Farrokh Gaffary's *Jonub-i Shahr* (South of the City), 1958, and Dariush Mehrjui's *Gav* (The Cow), 1969. Naficy explores the intermingling of Asian and Western influences and the social and political impact of this vibrant body of work. It is especially fitting to end with an essay on cinema, the newest artistic medium to cross Silk Road lands. •

Seven hundred years after Marco Polo, the Silk Road still evokes a fabulous geography that, like an ancient mariner's map, stretches between reality and fantasy. Indeed, these days the Silk Road is as much a product of imagination and metaphor as a legacy of history, and this very commingling is what makes it such an enduring symbol of cultural discovery and exchange.

Both the symbolism and the reality of the Silk Road attracted cellist Yo-Yo Ma, who founded the Silk Road

ONE • A CONVERSATION WITH YO-YO MA   YO-YO MA AND THEODORE LEVIN

Project, Inc. as a way to study the global circulation of music and musical ideas and to explore ways that traditional cultural expression can help revitalize contemporary culture. In 1999, Ma invited Theodore Levin, an ethnomusicologist and Central Asia specialist at Dartmouth College, to serve as the Silk Road Project's executive director. The following conversation between Ma and Levin took place in winter 2001, as the Silk Road Project launched a series of concerts and collaborative festivals to bring cross-cultural music making to audiences around the world (figs. 1.1, 1.2).

Detail, fig. 1.4. Plectrum guard, five-stringed lute, Japan, 8th century

LEVIN: In 1998, you founded the Silk Road Project to study the flow of ideas among different cultures along the Silk Road and to illuminate the living arts of peoples of Silk Road lands. Your interest in the Silk Road did not, I think, begin as a scholarly involvement. It came out of your own life experiences. Could you talk a little bit about this personal journey?

MA: I probably have to start about twenty-five years ago when my experience taking a liberal arts curriculum as an undergraduate opened many new worlds for me. It's almost as if everything that I do now has a reference point to those incredible years when I was stimulated by anthropology classes, history classes, a broad range of courses—not just music courses. I feel I am definitely a product of a liberal arts education, and I've benefited so much from that.

LEVIN: You have talked often about how those anthropology courses led you to visit and study the music of the Kalahari bushmen in Africa and how, even as you pursued your career as a musician immersed in the classical Western concert repertoire, you were interested in all kinds of music making.

MA: I have had lots of extraordinary teachers in my life. Two recent teachers are the violinist and fiddler Mark O'Connor and the bass player Edgar Meyer, both wonderful musicians. Mark and Edgar introduced me to Appalachian music, which has been influenced by musical traditions from Ireland, from Scotland, and from Scandinavia. They took me from a world I knew quite well, that is, the world of the classical cello, and led me into a new world, where, as part of a different fiddling tradition, I play my cello quite differently.

But it wasn't so easy to learn how to do this. The cello is a technologically complicated instrument that sounds great in a two-thousand- to three-thousand-seat hall. When I played with a lot of bravado, Mark said, "No, you can't do that." And when I tried to put a lot of coloring in, he said, "No, that doesn't work. Let's get to something more pure, more basic." So I had to learn an older style of intonation that was not familiar to me. The biggest challenge had to do with tempo. The cello is trained to respond but not at the speed that Mark plays. I had to learn to move my positioning of the bow. So now I can get into a fast Texas groove, but I had to make both mental and physical adjustments to do that.

Apart from the actual fiddling itself, one of the most useful things that Mark taught me was the importance of oral traditions in which music is transmitted, but also changed, through emigration and diaspora. For example, eighteenth- and nineteenth-

1.1 Yo-Yo Ma playing the Mongolian horse-head fiddle (*morin khuur*), 2001. Photograph by Elizabeth ten Grotenhuis

1.2 Theodore Levin, © Cylla von Tiedemann, 2001

century immigrants from Anglo-Celtic lands brought their jigs, reels, and hornpipes to the New World, where successive generations of musicians transformed them into a range of different styles and repertoires. These days, there is little common ground between the repertoires of, say, a Texas fiddler and a fiddler from Ireland, yet the two traditions reveal an unmistakable kinship. So I started thinking about how music sometimes stays the same and how it sometimes changes. I began to wonder what actually makes music change.

LEVIN: Did learning the Appalachian fiddling tradition affect your cello playing?

MA: Yes. Each time I learn a new style, I tend to internalize sounds of that style, which can then appear in my cello playing, as one more expressive component of musical communication.

LEVIN: There are certainly many different bowed instrument traditions in Asia, many of them interconnected. Can we move to that part of the world, the massive piece of earth stretching from the Mediterranean to the Pacific Ocean that has become identified with the Silk Road? What led you to Asia?

MA: A number of chance occurrences drew me to that part of the world. One of them was a trip to Jordan with some friends right after the peace treaty between Israel and Jordan was signed in 1994. We went to see Petra, a wonderful city with magnificent stone monuments, the terminus of a great caravan trade two thousand years ago, and we tried to figure out why the city was so wealthy for so many years. It's because they taxed everyone who traveled through.

That got me thinking about trade links in this part of the world. Then we met King Hussein and Queen Noor and, on the spur of the moment, Queen Noor asked me to give a master class in Amman the next day, on the way back to Tel Aviv. In that master class, I met some kids who were so passionate about music, who spoke about music in such poetic ways, that it made me think I had to learn more about these young people, understand their driving forces, do something to encourage their talents. And there were kids just like that in Israel and other parts of the Middle East. This early, chance encounter led to the formation of the Middle Eastern Youth Orchestra, under the direction of Daniel Barenboim. In addition to making wonderful music, the members of the youth orchestra are forces for peace and communication in this often-contentious part of the world. How did you become involved with Islamic music?

LEVIN: I also started in the European classical musical tradition. I did piano as a kid and also in college, but when I was twenty years old, I realized I wasn't going to be a concert pianist. So I decided to follow another interest and went to Israel to search for my spiritual roots, which are in Judaism. Wandering around the streets of East Jerusalem, I discovered, not Judaism, but Islam. It all had to do with hearing the sound of the muezzin.

MA: What's that?

LEVIN: The person who chants the Islamic call to prayer from the top of the minaret, the tower on a mosque. That sound may be one of the most distinctive sounds made by humans. It's a very finely etched, highly embellished cry to God. Hearing that sound changed my life, and ever since I've been studying the cultures of Islam. That sound started me on a journey that's still going and moving continually eastward.

MA: But you haven't given up your Jewish roots.

LEVIN: No. They've been enriched because I now understand their deep connection to other cultures that have shared the same territory. Understanding this connection, in

1.3 *Sufi dance* from a manuscript of the *Divan* by Hafiz. Present-day Afghanistan, Herat, dated 1523. Opaque watercolor, gold, and silver on paper, 18.8 x 10.3 cm. Freer Gallery of Art, Smithsonian Institution, Washington, D.C., purchase F1932.54. Inscription in upper right, translated by Wheeler Thackston (1990), reads: "Undo your tresses and make the sufi play and dance, for from every patch on his cloak you can shake thousands of idols."

fact, has led me to study the Bukharan Jews in Central Asia who have lived peacefully as a minority among Muslims for a thousand years.

MA: So when you say you discovered Islam, do you mean you discovered the religion, the culture, the music? In what ways do you mean that?

LEVIN: I mean all of those things because they're all linked. My entry into Islamic music and culture was through chant and sacred music and through learning about the Sufi ceremonies of the dervishes in Turkey (see fig. 1.3). I followed this tradition into Central Asia and began studying the classical musics of Central Asia that are inspired by Islamic metaphysics and aesthetics. Let me ask you what led you to the specific focus of the Silk Road?

MA: The art historian Elizabeth ten Grotenhuis told me about an incredible eighth-century Japanese collection called the Shosoin collection, in Nara, Japan, which reflects the arts of the Mediterranean world, Iran, India, Central Asia, China, Korea, and Japan. The collection includes painting, sculpture, lacquer ware, ceramics, calligraphy, swords, furniture, Buddhist altar fittings, perfumes, medicines, musical instruments, dance costumes, and masks. As luck would have it, I was taken to see this collection soon after, when I was visiting Japan with Milo Beach, then director of the Freer and Sackler galleries in Washington, and Charles Beare, the luthier and instrument specialist from London.

I was, of course, fascinated by the musical instruments, especially the pear-shaped lutes—called *biwa* in Japanese or *pipa* in Chinese. A five-stringed lute in the Shosoin collection is the only lute of this sort in Japan (fig. 1.4). The design on the plectrum guard, underneath the strings where the plectrum falls, evokes the Silk Road and its camel caravans. This plectrum guard is a band of tortoiseshell inlaid with a mother-of-pearl design of an Iranian figure riding a camel and playing a four-stringed lute. Of course, camels were unknown in Japan, so I can imagine how exotic this instrument looked to eighth-century Japanese. Several four-stringed lutes in the Shosoin collection are similar to ones still played today. I was fascinated by the *biwa* with a plectrum guard showing a group of entertainers riding on the back of an elephant in the midst of a mountainous landscape (fig. 1.5). This scene must have also seemed excitingly strange to Japanese people in the eighth century. There were, of course, no elephants in Japan, and the four entertainers themselves suggested foreign lands. An Iranian figure with a big nose and beard plays a hand drum while two youthful Chinese-looking musicians play transverse flutes to accompany a dancer with long sleeves billowing in the breeze. By the way, Elizabeth Barber writes about the appearance of these long sleeves on the Silk Road (see Chapter 3).

I think part of what I do as a musician is think about the imagination in a disciplined way. What do I know? What don't I know? I think musicians need to delve into the inner lives of composers and other musicians to figure out who they are and then to advocate and represent them. You are also an advocate for the musicians about whom you write in your book, *The Hundred Thousand Fools of God: Musical Travels in Central Asia (and Queens, New York),* which for me became one of the inspirational forces behind the Silk Road Project.

LEVIN: Advocacy is certainly one of the key elements of what I do as a music scholar. For example, in the book you mention, my aim was not simply to describe music in Central Asia but to get inside the lives of the extraordinary musicians I met there—people who don't necessarily have great currency in the global cultural marketplace but whose musical mastery and musical philosophy, if you will, make them very special. To write about these musicians, I found that I had to abandon conventional scholarly forms. My book is ethnomusicology disguised as travelogue. So your experiences in Jordan and Japan, reading my book—all this led to your founding the Silk Road Project in 1998?

MA: Yes. Up until then, I looked at lots of little pieces of information and said: aren't these interesting? And then I asked myself whether we could start to connect all those little dots. Could we actually do research and find vibrant traditions linking different parts of Asia, linking Asia and the West, linking past and present, that we didn't yet know about? Certainly from my own work with fiddlers and in looking at musical traditions in other parts of the world, I feel there are wonderful traditions that are worthwhile to discover, encourage, and celebrate.

LEVIN: Then you organized several conferences bringing together scholars and musicians and other people to see if such a project focused on Silk Road lands would be viable?

MA: Yes, and there were other, often spontaneous events that were as positive and encouraging as the conferences. I was talking earlier about learning the Appalachian fiddling tradition. I was introduced to a Mongolian fiddle in Amsterdam. We heard that there were four Mongolian musicians who had driven ten thousand kilometers in seven days from Ulaanbaatar, the capital of Mongolia, to Amsterdam. They had been living in Amsterdam for a couple of months playing music on the street. One night they came

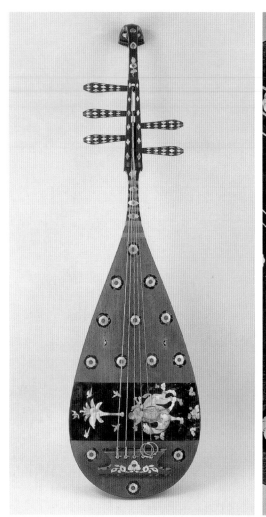

1.4. Five-stringed lute (*Gogen-biwa*). Japan, 8th century. Red sandalwood with tortoiseshell and mother-of-pearl inlay. Length 108.1 cm; width at plectrum guard 30.9 cm. Shoso-in Collection. Courtesy of the Shoso-in Treasure House, Nara, Japan

Detail, fig. 1.4. Plectrum guard. Tortoiseshell and mother-of-pearl inlay

and played for us and introduced us to the *morin khuur,* a two-stringed fiddle with a horse-head carving on the end of the scroll (see fig. 1.1). We had a wonderful evening, and they started to teach me how to play the horse-head fiddle. It's a beautiful instrument, but really hard to play. We were so impressed by their playing that we invited them to come and share my recital the next day, which they did. They appeared on the concert stage dressed in Mongolian clothes, and they played fabulously. I think everybody in the hall went crazy. So now we are studying music of the historical Silk Road, and we are commissioning new compositions from composers in Silk Road lands. We are exploring all sorts of musical and cultural connections and convergences in this enterprise.

LEVIN: But it seems to me that there is really a major difference between, on the one hand, looking backward as a historian on the kinds of cultural convergences that have taken place and the kinds of artifacts they've produced and, on the other hand, actively

designing and shaping those convergences ourselves. Are we trying to continue the tradition of the Silk Road and its forging of cultural convergences? Do we run the danger of creating convergences that may in retrospect seem forced or artificial in comparison to the convergences that took place over hundreds of years as a result of people's acknowledgment of what was really necessary? Why did objects, ideas, cultures move back and forth between East and West along the Silk Road? Wasn't it because in some sense people wanted them, either through fashion, or through economic necessity, or through a kind of aesthetic appreciation for the exotic? Isn't that different from someone saying, okay, I'm going to take a little of ingredient A and a little of ingredient B and mix them together and see what happens? These are some of the questions all of us involved in the Silk Road Project have to ask ourselves.

MA: I think it is legitimate for us to try to see what we can find out, to see if we can forge old and new knowledge. People may not know where something comes from.

1.5 Lute (*biwa*). Japan, 8th century. Sappanwood-stained maple wood with leather, pigments, gold leaf, tortoise shell, and mother-of-pearl inlay. Length 97 cm, width at plectrum guard 40.5 cm. Shoso-in Collection. Courtesy of the Shoso-in Treasure House, Nara, Japan
Detail, fig. 1.5 Plectrum guard. Pigments (white, black, red, green) and gold leaf on leather

33

Sometimes C may think that something comes from B, but may not know that it actually comes from A. And if you can establish that, in fact, certain parts of B come from A, then A becomes connected to C. That's new knowledge. That's important knowledge because A and C may not know they're connected. But, actually, they share a common tradition. In our world where people seem increasingly interested in finding their own identities, their cultural roots, sometimes we can get into trouble by saying my roots have no connection with your roots and therefore we're separate. But if we uncover the knowledge which shows that in fact there are connections, for example, between your Jewish roots and Islamic traditions, as you said earlier, this can be very liberating and incredibly valuable for cross-cultural understanding. If what you think is based on old knowledge as well as new knowledge, then you actually have to rethink things. I think that's very valuable for everybody. And it is equally valuable if we create artistic works based on the new knowledge we have uncovered, making these connections in a presentation or in a new musical composition.

LEVIN: In other words, you're saying that your feeling of freedom to connect different aspects of tradition is informed or legitimized by the actual history of these traditions in which connections that may not be apparent to us now did exist? Are you trying to recover lost aspects of tradition and use them as bases for new kinds of convergences?

MA: Some people engaged with the project are trying to recover this earlier knowledge. I'm trying to learn and to share whatever we learn with other people. As a musician, I feel that one of the things that I do when I perform is bring to audiences the totality of my experiences. I am trying to put into sound form my experiences and the things that I have learned and that I have been taught. I don't know whether that's recovery, but it becomes part of our collective imagination. I think it's important to develop collective imagination because then we actually have a shorthand of communication.

LEVIN: We're trying to revitalize aspects of traditional culture in Silk Road lands and to look at the big picture as we try to create a new understanding of the way music and culture circulate in the world. What are the risks of doing a project like this? I mean, do we risk contaminating traditions that have survived up until now in a more or less authentic form?

MA: What do you think? Do you feel there's a danger?

LEVIN: I think there's a danger if you don't document and preserve your original sources. In other words, no one would advocate burning Bach's manuscripts because music has moved beyond Bach, beyond eighteenth-century counterpoint, and we don't need that anymore. Everyone understands that Bach's work is a seminal achievement and a resource for us and for the future and for musical forms that we can't even imagine yet. So we value the preservation of Bach as a living resource. And it's the same, I think, in these traditional cultures. Just as in biological evolution, they constitute part of the record of our civilization and as such they deserve to be documented and preserved in living, active forms, not as museum pieces. Traditions are born and traditions decline and die when they're no longer useful to people. I think we want traditions to move forward. We want to innovate and encourage the creation of new forms of art and music that nourish the needs of the present and of young people and of their vision of the world. And at the same time we want to make people aware of their cultural heritage, which is in the traditions of the past.

MA: We seem to have two main jobs—to investigate and give credit to the past, on the one hand, and then to encourage new kinds of cultural development, on the other. All cultures evolve. And since we're more and more connected in this global world, we can't say, well, we'll keep something separate. That is certainly one way to kill cultural expressions very quickly. Look at the development of instruments, for example, how technology continuously allows for the updating of instruments for society's needs for musical performance. There seem to be certain moments when we need to delve very deeply into our specialties, and there are other times when we need to be really good generalists. I think this is a moment in time when it's appropriate to bring specialists together to see whether we can find a consensus about common knowledge that will enrich our own specialties. Otherwise, I think we could just dig ourselves into deeper and deeper specializations without really communicating with other people. That's one of the reasons that we got together, because we actually found that there's greater strength in working together with other people as we explore, seek, and learn.

LEVIN: I agree. But let's discuss this idea of local traditions and authentic convergences a little more. In the time of the Silk Road there was no question about the distinction between East and West. There was a geographical East and a geographical West and a cultural East and a cultural West. And there was exchange, and there was appropriation, and there were technology transfer and cultural transfer. But these days when we evoke the metaphor of the Silk Road for this East-West exchange, does it still make sense to talk that way about East and West? Do you feel that it still makes sense to talk about East and West in music?

MA: It depends on the individual. Some people will think so and some people won't. I think the way you talk about this issue in your book is very useful, that is, that East and

West can meet in Amsterdam, in London, in Cologne, in New York, in San Francisco, in Toronto. But let's make this discussion personal for a minute. We can talk abstractly about the past, about other cultures. Let's talk about us for a second. Do you find any dangers in working with someone like me? Do you feel that there is a danger of my appropriating your knowledge and distorting it because I am a performer and the non-scholarly part of me will say, I'll take anything you have and I'll use it to make a musical point, a statement, an event. Do you feel that there could be a degradation of your knowledge through working with someone like me?

LEVIN: It all comes down to a matter of taste and of trust. And I think in the abstract, yes, there could be a danger because if people's aesthetic choices are not informed by good taste or respect, then they could use traditional material in a way that degrades it. I have to admit that I sometimes worry about this as a scholar whose first commitment is to try to amplify the voices of the people for whose music I advocate, people who don't really have much voice in our world these days. I want to make sure that their voices are heard and that their ideas about music are put forward in the ways that they would wish rather than just have their music used as a resource for other people to make new creations and sell them in the global marketplace.

I don't worry about this with you because I trust that you come to these traditions with a sense of respect and awe and acknowledgment. You're committed to advocating for these traditions in their own form, for instance, in some of the concerts that we're doing, where a traditional Mongolian "long song" singer performs an authentic long song in a newly commissioned musical work inspired by the long song. For me this is exactly the right balance because the performance both preserves and advocates for the old while it shows at the same time how tradition can be used as a resource for innovative collaboration and creation. And it's all done with wonderful taste and respect, if I may say so.

I think that when we look at great musicians, they're the people who understand, who somehow figure out what the rules are and then how to go beyond these rules. That's what seems to me to be the engine that makes music continually evolve, makes it continually a mystery, makes me, for instance, want to go yet a hundred more kilometers into the Uzbek steppe because there may be something there that I never heard before that's going to change the way I think about music, or there may be a composer there from whom we might commission a work for the Silk Road Project.

MA: For me, one of the things that stimulates both scholarship and creativity is new knowledge. In this project we're on a steep learning curve because we're constantly faced with the unfamiliar—whether different cultures, languages, musical instruments, or disciplines. All that I'm learning will certainly change the way I play the cello, and it will change the way I think about the world. What's important is to start from inner knowledge and experience. Whatever our project contributes—new works, authentic convergences, innovative exchanges—will come from understanding music, people, and culture from the inside. •

My heart beat faster when the plane began its descent

toward Xining Airport on the Qinghai-Tibet Plateau.

I was nervous. I had spent more than seven years here

during the Cultural Revolution (1966–76), working with

the province's music and dance troupe. Qinghai, where

historically only exiles and prisoners lived, has always

been considered inhospitable. My life here had been

rough and difficult. It was not until Mao Zedong

(1893–1976) died and the Cultural Revolution was over

TWO • MELODIC MIGRATION IN NORTHWEST CHINA BRIGHT SHENG

that I returned to Shanghai to study music composition

at the Shanghai Conservatory of Music. Four years later I

moved to New York City to further my studies. I never

looked back.

When I left Qinghai in 1978, bringing to an end my

self-imposed exile, I sensed envy and perhaps jealousy

from some friends and colleagues. Now, twenty-two years

later, what would people think of me, especially since I

had not kept in touch? Would they still welcome me as

a friend?

But my heart had never left Qinghai. Although I

was born and raised in Shanghai, Qinghai always felt like

Detail, *Seated Musician*, China, Kizil, Xinjiang Province, Tang dynasty, 618–907. Pigment on stucco, 38.2 x 36.2 cm. Arthur M. Sackler Gallery, Smithsonian Institution, Washington, D.C. gift of Arthur M. Sackler, S1987.265. This musician is playing a lutelike instrument. See also figs. 1.4, 1.5, and 4.1.

a second homeland. I arrived when I was fifteen. It was here that I made up my mind to be a musician. It was here that I first kissed a girl. And it was in the mountains of Qinghai that I first tasted the beauty of the folk songs that remain the inspiration for my works. During the past two decades, I often dreamed of coming back to see my friends and smell the air in Xining, the capital, in my memory always dusty and filled with the odor of yak butter.

My specific purpose for returning to Qinghai was to study music cultures in this remote area in relation to the history of the Silk Road. In recent years I had become fascinated by the magnitude of commercial, cultural, and religious exchange the Silk Road had fostered among the countries between Asia and Europe. I wondered how music cultures moved along this route and how foreign music influenced, infiltrated, and embedded itself into Chinese music. I wondered if these interactions might have resulted in the distinct discrepancies between the music of northwest China and the rest of Chinese folk or classical music. And I wondered if it was still possible today to find traces of this ancient music migration in the modern-day Silk Road lands. In the summer of 2000, I finally made my trip. For two months I studied the music cultures of the Silk Road within the current Chinese border from Xi'an to Kashgar.

QINGHAI AND *HUA'ER* The worry about my reception turned out to be unnecessary. Many of my friends showed up at the airport to greet me, and I was adorned with a *hada*—a white silk scarf on which in ancient times a list of gifts would have been written—the highest honor of Tibetan culture (fig. 2.1). (The province of Qinghai used to be part of Tibet and was called Eastern Tibet. In Chinese, the word for Tibet is *Xizang,* meaning "western Tibet.") Xining has changed a great deal, too. The smell of yak butter is gone, and newly planted trees and high buildings give this remote provincial capital a fresh, friendly appearance.

Qinghai, named after a large salt lake within its border, was not originally part of the Silk Road. But when warlords and robbers made travel through the narrow Gansu Corridor impossible, trading caravans took an alternate route to northern Gansu via the Qilian Mountains in eastern Qinghai. The music culture in the region reflects its history (see fig. 2.2).

One of eastern Qinghai's most cherished musical treasures is *hua'er* (flowers), a form of love song heard only in the fields and mountains because of its zestful, often erotic content. My first destination was a *hua'er* festival in Huzhu, an autonomous county of Tu people three hours north of Xining by car.

2.1 Bright Sheng adorned with a *hada* at the Xining airport, 2000

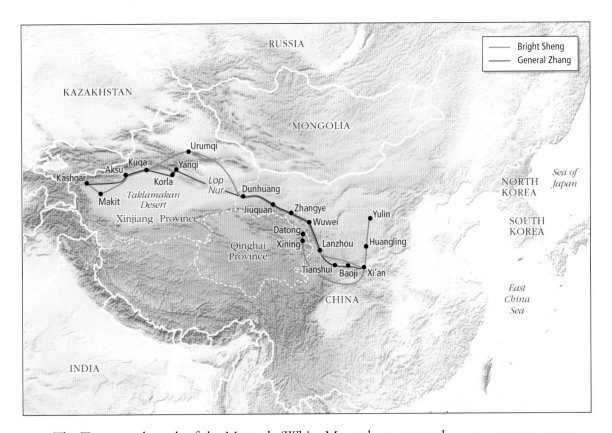

2.2 Map of Bright Sheng's route, 2000

The Tu were a branch of the Mongols (White Mongols, as opposed to the Yellow Mongols of Genghis Khan, ca. 1167?–1227). It is believed they had a dispute with their ruling authorities during the Ming dynasty (1368–1644) and migrated to Qinghai, then ruled primarily by the Tibetans. The Tu have a purely spoken language, a mixture of Mongolian and Tibetan, and they practice Tibetan Buddhism. Musically, Tu *hua'er* has a kinship with both Mongolian and Tibetan folk music. Tu *hua'er* singing uses a large throaty vibrato reminiscent of Mongolian singing. Its well-known dramatic movements, beautifully curved melodies that go straight up and down in large intervals, are reminiscent of Tibetan folk songs.

Hua'er is usually initiated by a young man, and if the object of his interest responds by singing her admiration back to him, the song can continue for quite a while—sometimes until well after dark, when the lovers really move into action. Extramarital affairs are commonplace during *hua'er* festivals but are usually forgiven as passing indiscretions. The *hua'er* festival is an event that local patrons have anxiously awaited throughout the year.

This year the festival took place in aspen woods along the banks of a dried river in Danma, a small town in Huzhu Province surrounded by mountains (fig. 2.3a,b). During the three-day festival, young men and women, dressed up in their finest clothes, wooed each other with love songs. One afternoon, when the day was at its hottest, the festival was also at its zenith. Standing in the middle of the riverbed, I had the overwhelming

2.3 a, b *Hua'er* festival held by Tu people

experience of being in a "*hua'er* ocean," as Qinghai is nicknamed. When all of the small groups sang different *hua'er* tunes in the same key by chance, the sound of one melody falling as the other was rising— enhanced by echoes from the valley, formed a truly remarkable polyphonic composition. Later, the sounds of many groups singing in different keys from different parts of the valley— swelled in Charles-Ivesian cacophony—but enlarged a thousandfold—and transformed music and nature into a masterpiece no composer could have written.

One of the earliest explorers on the Silk Road was General Zhang Qian of the Han dynasty [206 B.C.E.–220 C.E.]. Ever since the Warring States period [480–221 B.C.E.], the Chinese had been in constant military conflict with the Xiongnu, along China's northern borders. The Xiongnu—Huns of Turkic descent, some believed to be the ancestors of modern-day Hungarians—were militant and aggressive. Their actions prompted the Qin emperor Shihuangdi [ruled 246–209 B.C.E.] to build the Great Wall. Chinese sericulture was in full bloom by the time Wudi, the sixth Han emperor, ascended the throne in 140 B.C.E. Wudi was himself ambitious and had the desire to broaden the Chinese frontier. He sent Zhang westward with a caravan of one hundred men to form alliances with Xiongnu enemies, specifically the Yuezhi people, who had just been defeated by the Xiongnu in the north and driven to the southern edges of the Taklamakan Desert. Thus Zhang and his men bid farewell to their families, left the safe capital of Chang'an (now Xi'an), and started a dangerous and arduous trip.[1]

THE CITY OF XI'AN AND QIN OPERA The next province I visited was Shaanxi and its capital, Xi'an (formerly Chang'an), where General Zhang started. For some eleven hundred years, Chang'an, meaning "Forever Peace," was the capital under numerous Chinese emperors. The Tang dynasty (618–907), arguably the most sophisticated period of Chinese civilization, was its last and most prosperous era. At the time, Chang'an, with a population of two million, was the largest, most cosmopolitan city in the world. After Zhang Qian's discovery of the Silk Road routes to and from China, caravans of traders from western regions began arriving regularly in Chang'an. By the eighth century, this great metropolis had attracted foreigners from all over, including merchants, entrepreneurs, diplomats, pilgrims, sages, entertainers, and artists. In addition to Buddhism, the most influential religion at the time, other religions thrived in Chang'an. Nestorian churches and Zoroastrian temples were built during the seventh and eighth centuries. Islam, Judaism, and Manichaeism were also visibly present. At the Tang court, foreigners, including many musicians, held high official posts, and exotic costumes were the vogue. It is said that at its peak, there were more than twenty thousand non-Chinese living in Chang'an. With a stable economy and a foreign policy of openness, a great civilization took shape. Literature and poetry, calligraphy and painting, music and dance flourished at all levels of society, pre-dating European romanticism by more than a millennium.

But what would I find in today's Xi'an (Western Peace), now the capital of Shaanxi Province? Would I still be able to hear the music of Chang'an's glorious legacy?

I found some of the answers in Qin opera, an old operatic form whose history can be traced back to the Qin dynasty (221–206 B.C.E.). Originating in Xi'an and sung in its dialect, Qin opera, like all Chinese classical operas, combines music, dance, and drama (fig. 2.4). The best actors are excellent in all areas—singing, acting, narration, and martial art—the first of these being the most crucial element. The dramatically charged singing music is divided into two categories: happy and sorrowful tunes. The happy tunes, commonly believed to derive from folk songs of Shaanxi and Gansu, are based on pentatonic scales (five notes in each octave), like most mainstream Chinese music. What fascinates me are the unusual sorrowful tunes which, I suspect, are older and may have a closer relationship to the music cultures of Central Asia and share many of their traits. These tunes are based on the scale of eight pitches in an octave, a phenomenon peculiar for Chinese music. Highlighting the exoticism, the sorrowful melodies emphasize the dissonant intervals of the scale—tritones and major and minor sevenths and ninths. There are other similarities, too: microtonal pitch bending and the fiercely heartfelt singing style that sometimes resembles shouting more than singing.

The evolution of the Qin opera orchestra also points to interactions among Silk Road cultures. Lutelike (plucked) instruments, whose invention seems to have arisen in a number of early civilizations around the globe, were the first musical instruments brought into China via the Silk Road. *Pipa* (*biwa* in Japanese) and *sanxian* (*shamisen* in Japanese), two early descendants of the lute family, were the original lead instruments in

43

2.4 Qin opera performance

Qin opera. *Xiqin,* a bamboo-bowed *sanxian,* emerged during the Song dynasty (960–1279) and became the chief accompanying instrument. Eventually, the *xiqin* was replaced by the *banhu,* a louder and more flexible horse-hair bowed fiddle. It is thus natural that, in the instrumental interludes, one often hears fragments of musical traditions that apparently came from lands west of ancient China. Aside from *banhu,* the present-day Qin opera orchestra consists of *erhu* (two-stringed fiddle), *pipa,* bamboo flute, and an assortment of percussion.

The story of Yulin singing exemplifies how migration changed music practice. In northern Shaanxi, by the Great Wall and the Mongolian border, is an old military town called Yulin. Yulin was an important defense post, but the cold weather and harsh environment made it a place of exile for disfavored officials from the capital. One of them was General Tan of the Qing dynasty (1644–1911). Tan was originally from southern China, where it was stylish for wealthy families to have live-in female singers and musicians. After losing the favor of Emperor Kangxi (reigned 1662–1723), Tan was appointed governor of Yulin, and he moved there with his large family, including the musicians. As he entertained lavishly in his house, the graceful style of singing and chamber music playing from southern China became fashionable locally. With the passage of time, Yulin singing eventually spread into the narrow streets of this remote frontier town and became entertainment for average citizens.

But the Chinese tradition of the region considered female entertainers taboo. Even today, Yulin singing is predominantly done by males singing falsetto in imitation of

2.5 Yulin singing, Yulin, Shaanbei

female voices. There I experienced something curious: the vocal part, full of large leaps and sung in Shaanbei dialect by the unnatural male falsetto, was in discordance with the style of the instrumental accompaniment. Here, the typical elegance of southern instrumental playing, with its small intervallic rises and turns, was juxtaposed with the characteristic folk-song singing style of northern Shaanbei—a combination strange to me but apparently loved by the people in Yulin. During the full three-hour concert arranged for my visit, a large crowd from the street poured into the small classroom of a primary school and listened quietly throughout (fig. 2.5).

Just as they left Chang'an and stepped into the Gansu Corridor, General Zhang and his men were captured by the Xiongnu, who were sovereign in the region. Zhang undertook his special mission in disguise as an envoy sent by the Han emperor. The Xiongnu were suspicious and kept him under close watch, though they treated him well and even provided him with a wife. Zhang stayed there for ten years and had a son.

GANSU CORRIDOR AND MOGAO CAVES   Proceeding on my journey after Zhang, with the Qilian Mountains to the south and the Gobi Desert to the north, I drove through the barren and desolate narrow strip called the Gansu Corridor, from the city of Lanzhou to Dunhuang—a fascinating experience. It was astonishing to see how their old cultural glory and opulence had completely vanished from the province, now one of the poorest regions in China. During the Silk Road age, this was the indispensable principal passageway for traders traveling west to reach the outskirts of the Taklamakan Desert in Xinjiang Province. Because of the lucrative commerce, caravan towns along the Gansu Corridor reached the peak of their economic and cultural prosperity by the time of the Tang dynasty. Thanks to the mixed ethnicities, performing arts, especially music, also progressed rapidly and flourished in the region. *Xiliang* music, a form blending music and dance styles of Central Asia and northwestern China, was later brought into the capital, Chang'an. It became the craze both inside and outside the palace walls, remaining popular for five centuries. Important literati wrote hundreds of poems about the exotic style of *xiliang* music, which included singing, instrument playing, and dancing.

> The songs and dances of *xiliang* music,
> Have disseminated all over the world
> For those who cherish and find comfort in them.[2]

In Wuwei, an old caravan town north of Lanzhou, the cultural bureau clerk laughed when I inquired about *xiliang* music. But I did not want to give up. One afternoon near a public square I found a small group of blind people entertaining the pedestrians, a local custom by which the blind can earn a living. Listening to a performance of *xanxiao,* a ballad music, I noticed that while the singer was singing in a 2/4 meter, the accompanying instruments, *erhu* and *sanxian,* were playing in 6/8, a typical dance rhythm of Xinjiang. This cross-meter created a sense of independence between the singing and the instrumental line—a rare occurrence in Chinese music. Could this be the remaining shred of old *xiliang* music, which was known for its dance forms (fig. 2.6)?

However, it was in the silence of the Mogao Caves in Dunhuang (see fig. 5.9), in front of the dazzling wall paintings, that *xiliang* music became vivid and alive to me.

45

2.6 *Xanxiao* singing, People's Square, Wuwei, Gansu Province

Dunhuang (Blazing Beacon), named after a line of fortified beacon towers of the Great Wall, had been the westernmost trading center for China since the beginning of the Silk Road. Not only was it an inevitable stop for the caravans traveling westward, it was also the first town inside China for those who sought comfort and safety after a long journey. To ensure the success of their business and safe return from the arduous journeys that lay ahead of them, pilgrims, traders, and merchants constructed inside the rock escarpment Buddhist cave temples that remain one of the wonders of the world. The Mogao Caves, with nearly five hundred grottoes and some forty-five thousand wall paintings, survived through nine dynasties. The paintings are remarkably fresh in appearance, thanks to the arid desert climate.

About 360 of the caves date from the Sui (581–618) and Tang periods. Many of the paintings in them depict scenes of the Western Pure Land—a paradise-like realm where the faithful are born after death. Since Buddhists believe that good music comes from celestial regions, almost every Pure Land picture has *apsarases* (flying celestials) playing various musical instruments. One can speculate on the evolution of performance practices of Silk Road instruments by chronologically following these musical figures. In the earlier grottoes, for example, the *pipa* was shaped very much like an Arab lute with a long, turned neck and pear-shaped body. Through the years, it gradually grew into something more like the modern *pipa*. The same can be said of the way the *pipa* was played: at the beginning it was plucked with a large plectrum, which was eventually replaced by fingernails. (A number of music scores with ancient notation—believed to be the *pipa* accompaniment to singing—were also found in the Mogao Caves. But despite the efforts made by various musicologists worldwide, a convincing way to translate these manuscripts has not been discovered. Still, there seems to be a consensus as to pitches, while scholars are widely divergent in interpretations of rhythm and meter.) Performance practice at the time can also be seen clearly in the murals depicting music and dance forms, especially in the Tang dynasty grottoes.

A typical painting of this Pure Land paradise shows the Buddha Amitabha (Chinese: *O-mi-to-fo*) seated in the center of a magnificent palace surrounded by hundreds of deities (see fig. 2.7). Directly below are musicians and dancers. The musicians, separated into two groups of eight to fifteen members each by the dancers in the middle, play a large collection of instruments of different national origins—*pipa, zheng* (zither), *konghou* (harp), flute, seashells, *sheng* (mouth organ), cow horn, panpipes, reed

2.7 Mural of Buddhist Pure Land dancers and musicians, Mogao Caves, Dunhuang

pipe (*suona*, a double-reed trumpet originating in West Asia), and a variety of percussion instruments (chimes, bells, drums, and the now-extinct large clappers). Thirty-five different kinds of drums appear in the murals. The number of dancers is small; usually two females appear in the rather small central area (since the third century, female duet dance had been popular along the western territories). Some of the dancing figures are so vivaciously painted, with their flowing dresses and flying ribbons, I could almost see their fast virtuoso twirling movements and hear the exciting prestissimo dance music. Strumming the *pipa* behind one's back while dancing is another feat few modern-day dancers would dare to duplicate.

The exhilaration represented by these heavenly scenes is well described in a Buddhist text:

> Thousands of deities under luminous skies,
> The rustling of zither and crystal chimes,
> The pung-pung beatings of the drums,
> The ravishing melodies and resonating clouds,
> The reverberation of the invigorating flutes,
> Are all in the splendor of our celestial realm.[3]

After ten years of captivity, General Zhang and the remainder of his force managed to escape from the Xiongnu and continue their imperial mission westward, along the branch of the Silk Road north of the Taklamakan Desert to the region of present-day Kashgar. When he finally arrived, Zhang found to his disappointment that the Yuezhi had contentedly settled down there and were no longer interested in fighting the Xiongnu—the Chinese were far away and the Yuezhi would not want to war with their immediate neighbors. Zhang stayed there for more than a year before returning to Chang'an, this time along the branch of the Silk Road south of the Taklamakan Desert. Once more, he was captured by allies of the Xiongnu, the Tibetans. Miraculously, he escaped again. Finally, after thirteen years, he returned to Chang'an and received a royal welcome from Emperor Wudi. Only one of the hundred men who left with Zhang accompanied him home.

Though he had failed in his mission for Emperor Wudi, Zhang brought back invaluable detailed information about the Thirty-Six Kingdoms in the Western Territories, as well as the earliest knowledge of the Roman Empire and the countries bordering the Mediterranean Sea.

> Please drink another cup of wine,
> As you will have no friends west of Yang Pass.[4]

In ancient China, there was a genuine sense of mystery and fear about the "Western Territories," the vast area west of Yang Pass, the last military post of the Great Wall eighty kilometers outside Dunhuang. Historically, the Chinese considered the region barbaric, and its ethnic inhabitants expressed animosity toward Chinese sovereignty. Even today, the province of Xinjiang (New Dominion) remains exotic and esoteric for most Chinese (figs. 2.8, 2.9).

2.8 Ruins of a beacon tower of
the Great Wall, Yang Pass

XINJIANG AND MUKAM MUSIC   My next stop was Urumqi, the capital of Xinjiang. Located in China's northwestern corner, Xinjiang today occupies one-sixth of the country's territory (three times the size of France) and is home to a dozen non-Chinese ethnic peoples.

2.9 Bright Sheng on the Silk Road ("Western Territories")

During the Silk Road era, the territory that is present-day Xinjiang was part of what was known to Chinese civilization as the "Thirty-Six Kingdoms," which also included lands that fall within the present-day nations of Iran, Iraq, Pakistan, Afghanistan, Kazakhstan, Kyrgyzstan, Tajikistan, and Uzbekistan. Xinjiang did not become a Chinese province until 1884, during the Qing dynasty, although parts of this area were briefly under Chinese suzerainty during the Han and Tang dynasties. As a result of nomadic traditions and warfare, the ethnic makeup of this region shifted many times until the Uyghur people moved in and became the largest population in the province.

The Uyghurs, a Turkic people whose origins have been traced to the Altai region of south Siberia, were once militarily powerful. In the second half of the Tang dynasty, when China was facing conflicts with Tibet, the Uyghur army was paid large sums by the enfeebled Tang court to fight its enemies. Around the ninth century, after its defeat by the Kyrgyz, some of the Uyghurs were forced to migrate southwest across the Tian (Heavenly) Mountains (fig. 2.10) and to settle in the oases surrounding the Taklamakan Desert, while others moved east and founded kingdoms in northern Gansu. The Uyghur language is close to Turkish, though one can also find traces of its connection to Mongolian.

Numbering more than six million in Xinjiang, Uyghurs are known among their Han neighbors for their skilled craftsmanship and astute business sense. But they are also especially celebrated for their rich musical traditions of singing, dancing, and instrument playing. It seems that almost every Uyghur can sing, dance, or play an instrument, and sometimes all three (fig. 2.11).

Although prepared, I nonetheless felt the cultural diversity in Xinjiang. I was invited to lunch at a Uyghur friend's apartment in Urumqi, a city that today combines old and new. After the meal, to my surprise and delight, my friend's two sisters started dancing in the rather small room to Uyghur folk music playing from a boom box. I was captivated by these two beautiful Uyghurs dancing just a meter in front of me. As the music continued prestissimo, the intensity of the dance magnified. One of the dancers was swirling so quickly that she almost blinded my view; I could only feel the breeze her spinning body generated. It was extraordinary to see them dance so gracefully in such a small space without touching one another. Suddenly, I realized what I might be witnessing: the twirling dance of *xiliang* music!

2.10 Tian Mountains of Xinjiang

Dance also plays an important part in *mukam,* an art-music tradi-

tion popular in Islamic cultures. Depending on the locale, *mukam* can be spelled *makam, magam, maqam,* or *mugham.* Related repertoires are called *dastgah* in Iran, and *nuba* in North Africa. Although *mukam* music exists in a number of unique forms, all *mukam* systems share common features of musical structure and are performed on similar instruments. (Based on evidence of similarities of structure, tuning systems, and instruments employed, some experts believe that Uyghur *mukam* is related to an old music form found in the area over a thousand years ago.) A legend popular in Xinjiang tells of how Uyghur *mukam* became world famous thanks to Amenisha, an imperial

concubine of the Yarkand Kingdom (1513–1677) near Kashgar, then the most powerful region south of Tian Mountains and one of the cultural centers of Central Asia.

2.11 Uyghur street musicians, Urumqi, Xinjiang

The legend tells the story of Amenisha, a thirteen-year-old virtuoso player of the *satar* (a long-neck bowed instrument) whose playing was accidentally heard by the Yarkand king during a hunting trip to Makit, Amenisha's hometown. The king, also a master of *mukam,* was so enchanted by her superb music and her beauty that he proposed to her and brought her back to his palace. Recognizing her musical talent and wanting to enhance it, he invited all the best *mukam* musicians in the world to perform in Yarkand. Musicians traveled all the way from North Africa and Central Asia to play *mukam* on the banks of the Yarkand River—one of the biggest *mukam* festivals that ever took place. Meanwhile, Amenisha spent months systematically collecting and notating the *mukam* music of her guests; thus the glorious sixteen Kashgar *mukam*s were born (only twelve are known today). The Uyghurs crowned Amenisha Queen of Mukam and today proudly believe that the Kashgar *mukam*s are the best in the world.

Many features in Uyghur *mukam* music resemble old Chinese classical music, such as *Tang daqu,* a large-scale musical form popular during the Tang dynasty. Both are built around the principle of the suite—a succession of individual musical items juxtaposed to create both continuities and contrasts of key, rhythm, and melodic character. Individual songs in both traditions typically proceed through sections set at different tempos, for example, slow-moderate-fast. In Uyghur *mukam,* the first adagio vocal section, typically meterless, is followed by a lengthy andante instrumental section, and the suite concludes with fast dance music. The same musical logic also shapes the long arias of Qin opera. Often, a long suite consists of many alternating sections of adagio and andante, but the fast dance music is always at the end. Each *mukam* can last from a few minutes to a few hours, depending on the occasion and the space in which the music is performed. The expressive mode ranges from sentimental to savage, and the ensemble size varies from a few people to a small orchestra of a dozen. Such flexibility makes *mukam* popular and fitting for any social occasion.

Before the government invested in building a bridge across the river in 1994, the only way to get to Makit, a small oasis Uyghur community on the bank of the Yarkand, was by ferry rafts made of sheepskin. Not much of modern civilization has assaulted this peaceful hometown of Amenisha, part of the ancient civilization known as *dolang*, which encompassed areas around the Yarkand River. Excellent peasant *mukam* musicians can still be found in every village. There I experienced one of the highlights of my trip.

At a Uyghur family dinner, a richly varied spread of food and drink, five peasants performed *dolang mukam* with rough and rugged homemade instruments: *tanbur* (long-necked lute), *satar, aijet* (two-stringed fiddle similar to the Iranian *kamanche*), *dolang rewap* (a lute with extra resonating strings, much like the Indian sitar), *kolong* (plucked dulcimer), and *daff* (hand drum). The singing style immediately reminded me of Qin opera; the loud and fiercely coarse microtonal singing sounded more like shouting. It was five hours before the main course, a whole roasted lamb, was brought to the table. Then there was dancing, hosts and guests alike joining in. By the time we finally left the house at two in the morning—all very drunk—we had been there for more than nine hours. The most astonishing thing was that for this entire time, the five *mukam* musi-cians, all in their sixties and seventies, continuously sang and played without much break. Most extraordinarily, their energy and vocal quality

2.12 Village peasants performing *dolang mukam*, Makit

never deteriorated, in spite of their ceaseless smoking and drinking. To this day, I can still hear the raw, extremely stimulating music of *dolang mukam* (figs. 2.12, 2.13).

ABOUT 190 KILOMETERS north of Xi'an, among the lush pine trees, sits the mausoleum of the legendary Huangdi (fig. 2.14). Huangdi (Yellow Emperor) is believed to have established the earliest Chinese monarchy in 2987 B.C.E., meaning that in the year of my visit it was the year of 4987 according to the Chinese calendar. During his reign of more than a century, Huangdi supposedly invented agriculture, the written Chinese language, politics, religion, philosophy, arts, medicine, music, and just about everything else in preserved modern civilization. His empress was the presumed discoverer of sericulture. Hailed as the founder of Huaxia (Chinese nation) and the ancestor of all native

Han Chinese (since the Han dynasty, ethnic Chinese are conventionally called "Han"), Huangdi is memorialized by a mausoleum, a holy shrine for all Chinese; yellow is the color of the earth, of the Yellow River, and of Chinese skin. Each year thousands of Chinese from around the world come here to worship and pay their respects.

2.13 Uyghur dinner, Xinjiang

On my way back from Shaanbei I, too, stopped for a visit. The experience turned out to be quite enlightening, but not for reasons I could have guessed. I first noticed that Huangdi's surname, Gongsun, is not a typical name for Han Chinese. Rather, it belonged to one of the minority ethnic peoples who inhabited the area at the time. I further observed that most of the ethnic peoples who lived under his reign were not consanguineous Han Chinese. I was rather baffled to realize that none of these facts were much discussed in Chinese communities and publications, though the information

2.14 Huangdi Mausoleum, Shaanxi Province

has been there all along. I suspect that most Chinese, like me, would not know that Huangdi was actually not a Han by blood. How could it be that for thousands of years the Chinese have been worshiping a non-Chinese as their original ancestor?

Maybe the Yellow Emperor should instead be considered the founder of Huaxia culture, which originated in northwest China, an area inhabited by many different ethnic groups since the dawn of Chinese civilization. Indeed, is there any nation in the world that is pure-blooded? Or any pure culture, for that matter?

It was remarkable to see so many different musical cultures pictured performing together in the Mogao Caves. During the Tang dynasty, the imperial court categorized Chinese music into ten genres to include music from Korea, India, Burma, and kingdoms of Central and West Asia like Bukhara, Samarkand, and Iran. Surprisingly, among the ten only two were genuine Chinese: *yanyue,* a lavish musical form for court banquets, and *qingshang,* traditional Chinese folk music. Today many Chinese scholars claim that this was part of a brilliant foreign policy carried out by Chinese emperors. The emperors seem to have been confident and secure that Chinese culture would absorb any foreign influences.

I think there might be other elements at play. The influence and attraction between powerful Chinese empires and surrounding countries were very much like the present-day relations between the United States and the rest of the world. I was over-whelmed to discover during my trip that American pop culture reached almost every corner of this remote area. In many of the small villages, I saw American soap operas on television, and in each town I could find street vendors selling pirated tapes of American pop songs. Still, I do not believe that someone is manipulating American pop culture in remote parts of the world. Instead, for better or worse, I could feel a natural attraction to American culture. In turn, American culture itself has been enriched deeply because of its diversity and inviting environment. As a result, what defines American music today is exactly this melting-pot effect—from European classical music to jazz, folk, pop, new age, Asian, and African music. This multiculturalization makes it possible for composers like American Lou Harrison, whose music shows strong Asian influence, and myself to have an audience.

Likewise, during the dynasties when China was economically and militarily powerful, young people from many countries went to study in China, and foreigners regularly lived in Chinese cities. While China assimilated foreign cultures, Chinese people also migrated throughout Asia.

On the flight back from China, I felt blessed. I am blessed that I lived in Qinghai and that I left for America to develop my musicianship. Wherever I live, Qinghai and northwest China will always be my homeland, a place to which I now feel closer than ever. But mostly, as a musician steeped in both cultures, I feel blessed that the Silk Road produced such a fantastic mixture of cultures—a beautiful gift to humankind. •

NOTES

The author wishes to thank Michael Rodman for coediting the essay, Mary Lou Humphrey and Deborah Horne for their first reading of the essay, and Wendy Lee for transcribing the vocal diary of the trip.

1   This is a retelling of a well-known story. L. Boulnois, *The Silk Road,* trans. Dennis Chamberlin (London: George Allen & Unwin, 1966), pp. 23–30. The retelling continues throughout this chapter and always appears in grey type.

2   Excerpted from Du Mu: (803–852) "He Huang Rivers," in *Collection of Ancient Poems on Liang Zhou,* Wuwei County Annals no. 3 (Gansu: Wuwei County Annal Editorial Office Press, May 1985) p. 105. Published in Chinese.

3   Qingbao Zhou, "The Subject Matters and Contents of Qiuci Wall Paintings," in *Researches on Silk Road Arts,* Quici Buddhist Civilization. Collection of Dunhuang Bianwen, vol. 5, (Xinjiang: People's Publisher, January 1994), p. 127.

4   Excerpted from Wang Wei, "Music of Weicheng," in *A New Annotation of Three Hundred Tang Poems,* annotated by Jing Xing Yao (Shanghai: Shanghai guji chubanshe, 1993), in Chinese, p. 373.

"Silk for glass! Silk for glass!"

Such might have been the cry of a merchant wending his way eighteen hundred years ago through the unfamiliar streets of Palmyra and Damascus, the silk goods he sought to trade having survived the nearly eight thousand-kilometer journey from northern China, across burning deserts, knife-sharp salt flats, and towering mountains, the caravan driver beset at every step by bandits, thirst, and weariness.

THREE • FASHIONED FROM FIBER ELIZABETH BARBER

SILK AND GLASS Somewhat before 2000 B.C.E., people in northern China discovered that they could harvest the silk of worms feeding on local mulberry trees by dropping the fresh cocoons into boiling water. This killed the larvae and dissolved the gum sticking the fibers together so one could find the end of the gossamer thread and unwind it—even to a length of a thousand meters. Only the northern Chinese species (*Bombyx mori* in its domestic form) can be unwound thus, because the cross-section of its thread is round, unlike that of other silkworms, and hence much stronger and less breakable.[1]

A Pair of Painted Pottery Female Dancers, China, Tang dynasty, see fig. 3.14.

3.1 Detail of Chinese chain-stitched silk embroidery of vine with phoenix or pheasant. The piece was later cut up, edged with felt, and made into a Central Asian saddlecloth. Pazyryk, mound 5, ca. 300 B.C.E. (after Sergei I. Rudenko, *Frozen Tombs of Siberia* [Berkeley: University of California Press, 1970, fig. 91])

By the time of the great Shang dynasty (ca. 1600–1050 B.C.E.), women serving the imperial households (for silk was a royal monopoly) had become adept at dyeing and weaving this silk into plain and patterned fabrics of surpassing loveliness. And by 400 B.C.E., tantalizing silk stuffs were reaching Europe via nomads wandering the long, narrow belt of grasslands, or steppes, stretching across Eurasia from Hungary almost to present-day Beijing. We know the nomads were carrying silk, because in one of their tombs, frozen by permafrost at Pazyryk in the Altai Mountains, eight hundred kilometers north of the later Silk Road, archaeologists found a saddlecloth of about 300 B.C.E. made from Chinese silk embroidered with colorful, pheasantlike phoenixes roosting in delicate scrolls of greenery[2] (fig. 3.1). Chinese annals record that much silk and occasional princesses were used to bribe the nomads to stop raiding the rich Chinese farmlands.[3] The phoenix being a royal bird, mythologically denoting the empress, ladies of the emperor's house would embroider it, and we may wonder whether this cloth came west with such a bartered princess. The ancient Chinese word for silk traveled west with these shimmering fabrics,[4] giving us our word *silk* and giving to the Greeks, whose Black Sea colonies fringed the western nomad lands, their word *sērik-ós*. Since *-ikos* was a common Greek ending meaning "belonging to," the Greeks decided that the first syllable must be the name of the originators of this strange cloth and adopted *Sēr, Sêres* as their word for the easternmost inhabitants of the world—China and the Chinese. It survives still in our term for raising silkworms, sericulture.

The Greeks fell in love with the new luxury. One ancient cynic even quipped that the ladies wanted silk so they could clothe themselves while appearing naked. By 100 B.C.E., when silks were starting to arrive in western Asia via India, Roman ladies were clamoring for it too, while western weavers sometimes made a living unraveling the heavy Chinese brocades and reweaving the luminous threads into finer webs.

During the Han dynasty (206 B.C.E.–200 C.E.), the Chinese had pressed hard to open a trade route to the West. They first broke through the Gansu Corridor into the desert basins of eastern Central Asia just before 100 B.C.E., and thence over and around the Tian and Pamir Mountains into the west. There they finally reached people who had the two magical items the Chinese most desired: "heavenly horses" and eye-dazzling glass.

Multicolored and delicate, and also a trade secret for millennia, glass was a fitting cultural rival for silk. It was probably first produced by the Sumerians nearly three thousand years earlier and likely by accident, since the fusion of quartz sand into glass requires melting the silicates at above sixteen hundred degrees Celsius and then cooling it very slowly, over many days.[5] (For comparison, the molten basalt that spurts and splatters like overheated pudding from the vents of Kilauea is some four hundred degrees cooler.) But once you have some old glass to drop in as catalyst, you can make glass happen at a far lower temperature, and colors can be had simply by adding various metallic oxides to the mix. Its basic manufacture long kept secret, glass was shipped out in bun-shaped ingots for other artisans to fashion into objects as needed. By Roman times, the secret was widely known in western Asia, Egypt, and southern Europe, but the greatest centers of glassmaking were still around the east end of the Mediterranean.

3.2 Weaver producing silk *ikat,* a fabric decorated by dyeing the threads (the warp, in this case) before weaving and by tying something tightly around the threads wherever the dye is not supposed to color the thread. Village near Kashgar, Xinjiang, 1994. Photograph by John Sommer

It was there in the Levant, in the first century B.C.E., just as the Romans were conquering the area, that a great revolution in glassmaking occurred: blowing the glass instead of molding or cutting it. This new technology allowed a whole host of fairytale forms with which to enchant the eye. The dainty, colorful new Roman glass made a fitting trade for delicate, many-hued Chinese silk (if not so easy to transport). And so the Silk Road was born—or perhaps the Glass Road.

Trade thrived. Townsfolk of the Tarim Basin had begun to clothe not just themselves but their dead in silk. For example, at Niya, on the southern branch of the Silk Road, one couple buried about 200 B.C.E. wore entire suits of colorfully patterned silk to the grave, their faces covered by large squares of fancy silk finished off with wide red edges.[6] Silk takes dye easily, and surely its colorfulness attracted buyers as much as its delicate feel (fig. 3.2). Cotton, though equally easy to dye, came to compete with silk only much later. Domesticated in the Indus Valley by 3000 B.C.E., cotton finally made its way to Assyria, Egypt, and Central Asia in the first millennium B.C.E. as a botanical curiosity and luxury import. A coarse variety suited to growing in desert conditions came to be cultivated around Turfan by 500 C.E., but cotton achieved importance in China only in the thirteenth century C.E., when a new variety reached Shanghai from humid Southeast Asia.[7] Until then, silk reigned as the supreme fabric.

Despite a royal Chinese decree that exporting live silkworms or mulberry seeds carried the death penalty, the smugglers eventually won, and whole avenues of mulberry

3.3 Toyuq oasis, just east of Turfan, in Xinjiang. Here a river of meltwater leaves its gorge through the Flaming Mountains (so-called because of their reddish orange color and desert heat) onto the desert flats, where it can be used for watering crops—principally grapes, melons, and mulberries. Tops of an avenue of mulberry trees can be seen in the green gully beside the blue-tiled mosque. The brick "cage" in the foreground is for drying grapes into raisins. Photograph by Elizabeth Barber

3.4 Women reeling silk from cocoons in a village near Kashgar, 1994. A huge cauldron of water set into a stove (lower right) is kept simmering over a fire (just visible at bottom). The hot water dissolves the gum seracin that holds together the silk cocoons visible floating on the surface. The woman squatting on top of the stove gathers several loosened ends of silk and begins pulling the filaments (visible in her left hand) off the cocoons, paying them out to be wound up onto a large reel turned by a helper (left). The threads are pulled in small groups both to speed the work and to reduce breakage, since a single filament may be as much as one kilometer long. A considerable mass of white silk can be seen on the rim of the wheel. Photograph by John Sommer

trees sprang up in towns the length of Eurasia to feed the precious worms that spun the equivalent of gold (fig. 3.3). I have walked down the descendants of many such avenues myself, from the great oases of Turfan and Urumqi (Ürümchi) to little Mediterranean ports like Siteia in Crete.

In Kashgar and Khotan, you can even see silk makers still at work in the old way. Kettles bubble as women reel the gossamer fibers off the floating cocoons (fig. 3.4); great skeins of freshly dyed silk—delphinium blue, dandelion yellow, hot pink—hang in the breeze to dry, bound with myriad other tiny threads at precise intervals to resist the dyebath in a future pattern. Tied thus, they look like long sausage strings of the cocoons they came from. Elsewhere, looms clack and shuttles fly as the ikat patterns emerge from their cocoons anew onto great banners of woven silk, to be sold to local patrons and tourists alike—to textile enthusiasts from the world around who have reopened a New Silk Road in search of the old.

WOOL But before there was silk, there was wool.

Some four thousand years ago, two millennia before blown glass, a woman who still retains an appealing beauty was laid out in a shallow, sandy grave on a river terrace overlooking the route of the later Silk Road, near where that faint track departs westward from the pitiless salt flats of Lop Nur and the now-dry oasis of Loulan, at the east end of the great Tarim Basin[8] (fig. 3.5). The woman's winnowing basket lay over her face, she wore a skirt and moccasins of hide plus a felt hood adorned with a large feather, and she was wrapped in a simple rectangle of woven wool, probably her cloak, fastened with a wooden pin. The wrap had extra loops of weft woven in as insulation to keep her warm. For although the area is desert—hot and parched in the summer—the winter temperatures get to thirty and forty degrees below zero. Her body and clothing, and even the grains of wheat in her little woven grass bag, were almost perfectly preserved by the dryness—but not summer dryness, for the heat would have caused decomposition to outrace desiccation. The cold-weather clothes tell us that she must have been buried in winter and that she freeze-dried, much like the Neolithic Ice Man (Oetzi) recently found on the Simplon glacier between Italy and Austria.

Most graves in Central Asia contain nought but bones. Yet here and there at the very center of the silk route, in the huge sandy bowls known as the Tarim, Turfan, and Hami Basins (today's Uyghur Autonomous Region), we find naturally mummified bodies with intact clothing, buried over the last four thousand years. Our Beauty of Loulan happens to be the earliest in this

3.5 *The Loulan Beauty,* painted by Kelvin Wilson, Rotterdam, 1997; a reconstruction of a four-thousand-year-old Central Asian mummy and her world. She wears a hide skirt and moccasins, an oblong blanket wrap woven of natural brown sheep's wool (secured with a wooden pin), and a felt cap with a feather. The primitive woolly breed of sheep she herded grazes behind her, and she is using a winnowing tray (found laid over her) to separate wheat from chaff. Her small woven-grass bag for storing wheat lies by her knee, along with the comb she probably used both for grooming and for preparing wool. Wheat and wool were both domesticated in the ancient Near East (West Asia) and must have been taken eastward by Caucasians such as this woman and her clan. They also prized ephedra (bush in background), apparently for the stimulant it contains. (Based on grave finds at Qawrighul, near Loulan [Uyghur Autonomous Region].)

unique series. A few other men, women, and children similarly attired and equipped show us that the earliest permanent settlers along the middle reaches of the Silk Road were Caucasoid immigrants from the west. Their clothing is simple: for women a skirt (either solid, or of strings like a skimpy hula skirt), a belt for men, and for both sexes moccasins for the feet, feathered hoods and caps for the head, plus an all-purpose blanket wrap. These newcomers cultivated wheat, a western plant first domesticated in what is now Syria; and they herded sheep, from which they obtained the wool for their hoods and blanket wraps.

Varieties of wild sheep live in several parts of the world, but the ancestors of the sheep from which we get wool were first domesticated in the Zagros Mountains, which lie along Iran's border with Iraq. Research shows that these sheep were not woolly when first tamed, however, and that it took millennia of inbreeding to develop usable wool. That step, too, took place in the vicinity of the Zagros, for woolly sheep began spreading from there around 4000 B.C.E.. Thus the wool in the desert mummies' clothing came to Central Asia on the backs of western sheep.

At 1000 B.C.E., the desert mummies are still invariably Caucasoid, with big noses, round eyes (probably blue), light brown to reddish blond hair, and heavy beards among the men. They still wear exclusively wool, but now they wear fitted clothing in lieu of blanket wraps.

Near Cherchen, along the southern leg of the later Silk Road, archaeologists found the mummified remains of a man, three women, and a baby, who had all died in rapid succession—presumably of something quickly toxic like *E.coli*. The best preserved of the women (fig. 3.6) wore a knee-length dress densely woven of bright red wool, while the man (fig. 3.7), reckoned to be about fifty-five, wore trousers and a long-sleeved shirt, all of eye-catching purply red-brown wool, with a multicolor belt cord. Both adults have red woolen threads through their earlobes, swirls of bright ocher on their faces (his yellow, hers red and yellow), and white deerskin boots to above the knee. The baby (fig. 3.8), wrapped in a blanket of the man's purply red-brown wool, wore a bonnet of brilliant blue felt edged with red. Small blue stones had been laid over its eyes.

The man's trousers were a recent invention. A century or two before, steppe nomads had started to ride right on the backs of their horses rather than using them only for pulling chariots, and trousers were devised to protect tender parts from chafing. Fashion, too, traversed Central Asia: the Chinese adopted pants around 400 B.C.E. when they took up horse riding to beat the marauding nomads at their own game. Obtaining yet swifter horses was in fact one of the emperor's chief objectives in opening the Silk Road in the second century B.C.E. The Cherchen family was well acquainted with horses, for their tomb contained both a saddle and horse bones.

HORSES AND CHARIOTS Horses had been tamed some three thousand years earlier in the Ukrainian steppes, but they were not much used at first. The earliest wheels invented were solid slices of log, and carts that had them were too heavy for horses to pull without the efficient trace harness finally devised in the fourth century B.C.E. Around 2000 B.C.E., apparently as a result of learning how to curve wood permanently

3.6 Below: Mummy of tall Caucasoid woman in red woolen dress and white boots, found at Cherchen along the southern branch of the Silk Road), dated to 1000 B.C.E. (Bronze Age). She has five braids (three of which are false switches), red and yellow face paint, and a chin strap intended to hold her jaw shut (it failed.) Urumqi Museum, photograph by Elizabeth Barber

3.7 Right: Mummy of tall Caucasoid man with yellow-ocher face paint and graying hair twisted into a queue, found in the same tomb as the woman in figure 3.6, Cherchen, 1000 B.C.E. Like the woman, he has red yarn through his earlobes and a chin strap of plaited, dark red wool, which in this case succeeded in keeping the mouth shut. Urumqi Museum, photograph by Irene Good

3.8 Lower Right: Mummified baby wearing a blue and red felt bonnet and wrapped in a purply red-brown baby blanket bound with a red and blue tie of twisted wool. Little blue stones cover its eyes, and wisps of orange wool close its nostrils. From Cherchen, 1000 B.C.E. Such intensity of color is startling for textiles so old, but the preservation may have been aided by the extreme saltiness of this cemetery. Urumqi Museum, photograph by Elizabeth Barber

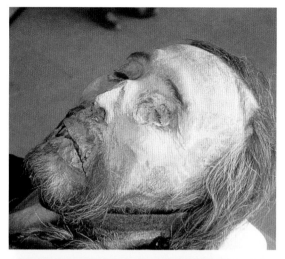

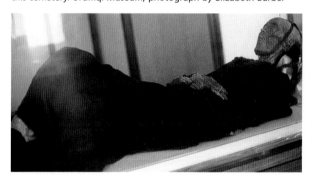

for better bows, people living where the steppes cross the southern Urals figured out how to curve wooden strips full circle around a set of radial struts, thus inventing the spoked wheel. This wheel was lightweight yet strong—mostly air, compared to a log slice. Harness a horse or two to a light chariot slung on a pair of spoked wheels, and off you go in the manner of Ben-Hur, faster than the wind.

Faster than the rest of the world, anyway, and that was what counted. Steppe warriors began to terrorize their neighbors, who had to acquire chariots of their own to compete, and so on in ripples that spread rapidly to both ends of Eurasia. The wave splashed into ancient West Asia about 1800–1600 B.C.E. Hittites and Mycenaeans with horse chariots took over in Turkey and Greece, while a riptide of chariot warfare surged down through the Levant to Egypt. There, to the horror of the Egyptians, foreigners called the Hyksos managed to invade the delta of the sacred Nile; and like the Chinese, the Egyptians took up the new technology to fight back.

Traveling eastward, the wave had farther to go, hitting China by 1200 B.C.E. Spoke-wheeled chariots and horses occur in the royal Shang dynasty burials near the ancient capital city of Anyang (five hundred kilometers south of Beijing, but still north

3.9 Three Bronze Age hats from Cherchen, ca. 1000 B.C.E. Left to right, red-brown woolen beret made in a looping technique with threaded needle; white felt helmet-shaped cap with hornlike roll of felt; brown felt peaked cap with yellow blanket stitch. Right, tall peaked woman's hat from Subeshi, near Turfan, 5th century B.C.E. (after *The Ancient Art in Xinjiang, China* [Urumqi: Xinjiang Art and Photography Press, 1994], pls. 253–54; James Mallory and Victor H. Mair, *The Tarim Mummies* [London: Thames and Hudson, 2000], figs. 111, 125)

of the Yellow River), while proof that the technology came from far to the west lies embedded in the vocabulary. Recent research demonstrates that the ancient Chinese words for *wheel, chariot, axle, nave,* and so on were borrowed from Indo-European languages, and most of them demonstrably from Iranian.[9] The connection is not a big surprise, actually, for we know that tribes speaking various Iranian tongues formed some of the principal groups of steppe nomads from at least 2000 B.C.E. on. Indeed, many of the local place-names that the Chinese adopted as they moved into Central Asia in 110 B.C.E. have Iranian etymologies.

More than horsemen, however, made it all the way to the Shang capital: a swarm of words to do with diviners and divination—an Iranian specialty—came into ancient Chinese from Iranian also. A few tiny sculptures have survived in northern China from the first millennium B.C.E., showing round-eyed, beaky-nosed foreigners wearing Persian-type tall "magician's hats" (our own words *magic, magician, Magi* also come from Iranian).[10]

Hats? Another Central Asian specialty. Cherchen Man had ten in his tomb (fig. 3.9), including needle-netted red-brown berets, a horned helmet of white felt, and a peaked felt hat rather like Robin Hood's. Brown with yellow buttonhole stitching, this last resembles the famous Phrygian hat (the Phrygians entered Turkey from the steppes about this time) that became a symbol of liberty in the Classical world and subsequently in the French Revolution, where it was depicted on the mythical "Marianne." No tall pointy black hats appeared at Cherchen, but just such have turned up in women's graves of 500 B.C.E. at Subeshi in the Turfan Basin. Clearly, fashions in clothing were already moving east and west the length of Eurasia long before the traditional Silk Road itself was established around 100 B.C.E.

TEXTILE TECHNOLOGY Textile technology was moving too. Cherchen Man's belt cord (fig. 3.10) was made in a multistrand plaiting technique called *kumihimo* in Japan, where it is still used. Such cords are made on a wooden stand, using spool-shaped weights to hold and tension the component threads, much as in lace making although on a coarser scale. Clay weights of suitable size, shape, and heaviness occur at many southern European sites, 4000–1500 B.C.E. Unfortunately there are too many holes in

3.10 Right: Belt cord on the male mummy from Cherchen, 1000 B.C.E. (see fig. 3.7), plaited with a technique still used as a traditional art in Japan today (called *kumihimo*). The shirt and pants were woven from natural brown wool dyed with red dye, giving an unusual purply red-brown color. Naturally pigmented wool is seldom dyed, but this same technique of applying red dye to brown wool is still used today for men's coats in Tibet. Urumqi Museum, photograph by Irene Good

3.11 Lower left: Woolen tapestry with interlocked red and yellow spirals, woven in a twill that jumps more than two threads at once to hide the warp and edged with a tricolored plaited band. From disturbed tomb at Cherchen, mid-1st millennium B.C.E. Urumqi Museum, photograph by Irene Good

3.12 Lower right: Jagged tapestry design woven in a warp-hiding twill between the red cuff and turquoise body of a large woolen shirt: Cherchen, mid-1st millennium B.C.E. Urumqi Museum, photograph by Irene Good

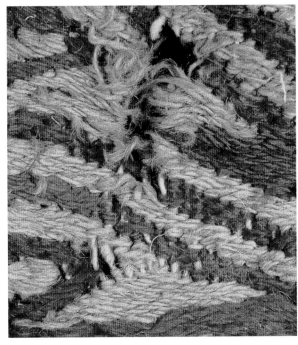

our data to determine which way this craft spread—or whether such plaiting was invented independently in East and West.

But the technique of tapestry, which apparently first developed in Syria in the third millennium, seems to have spread bit by bit from a single source. After chasing the Hyksos northward out of Egypt with their new horse chariots, the Egyptians returned home from Syria around 1475 B.C.E. with captive cloth workers, the tapestry loom, and tapestry technique. Nearly a millennium later, we see the idea of tapestry firing the imaginations of weavers in the Tarim Basin (figs. 3.11, 3.12). But only the idea came in, not the weavers with the know-how, for the locals accomplished the same effects as in "traditional" (weft-faced plain-weave) tapestry by using a peculiar local weave structure:

a twill in which the weft hops over three to five warps at a time.

Several early examples of this strange twill were found in the Cherchen family's tomb: two heavy overcoats, a baby blanket, and the woman's bright red dress. The dress, calf-length with long sleeves, sports pea green "piping" sewn down with small alternating black and white stitches and a very rudely sewn hem. The sleeves are set with the armpits left open, but this design is not just a makeshift before the invention of the gusset, for gussets were known. One pair of pants from this same tomb has a perfectly functional gusset in the crotch. The underarm hole improves ventilation, of course, but it also provides a slit through which to stick your arms so you can dive into such tasks as the laundry without undressing. Whatever its use, the feature has persisted in women's jackets in parts of Central Asia to this day, though the materials have changed. Jackets are now made up in bright, factory-woven velveteens, with store-bought cotton rickrack in place of homemade piping of wool.

LINEN   But even before there was wool, there was linen. And it was linen sleeves that launched one of the most remarkable fashions in clothing ever to traverse Eurasia and the Silk Road.

Linen comes from the bast or stem fibers of the flax plant. All our earliest remains of string and cloth, in fact, are of bast fiber, in the New World as well as the Old, and in China as well as western Eurasia. Flax grew wild in great stands in prehistoric western Asia, and the fiber that flax gives is finer and sleeker than that of most other plants. It was ideal for clothing—when people finally began to clothe themselves for status, toward the end of the Stone Age in the fourth millennium B.C.E.[11]

Linguistic evidence embedded in the history of the word "tunic" and its cognates, combined with archaeological finds, tells us that the linen tunic must have begun in the northern part of Mesopotamia. At first it was just a simple length of linen cloth wrapped around the body and over one shoulder; but as it traveled into the colder climes of Eastern Europe (word and all), it acquired two more squares sewn on at the sides to form sleeves: the original T-shirt. The earliest Central Asian mummies, like the Beauty of Loulan, wear a plain wrap, whereas the Cherchen adults, a thousand years later, have simple shirts, dresses, and coats with T-sleeves of this sort.

Having observed the invention of the basic T-sleeve, keep it in mind while we jump to China.

THE ULTRALONG SLEEVE   Highborn ladies in the traditional Chinese opera often punctuate a remark by flipping down an enormously long pair of silken sleeves, known as "water sleeves" for the way they billow. The gesture tends to carry an air of great finality with it, perhaps because the speaker's hands—those "windows to the soul" for performers—are now completely covered and inaccessible.

Such sleeves are not native to China but came via the Silk Road. They first appeared in China on monuments from the Han and Tang dynasties, the two periods when China was heavily involved with Central Asia. While the generals of the Tang dynasty (618–907 C.E.) reopened the Silk Road, carrying Chinese military conquests far to the west, the royal court spent its time fostering the arts—poetry, music, and dance—and developing a taste for exotica.[12] Central Asian musicians and dancers were particularly welcomed as entertainers, and their song and dance styles, whether vigorous or willowy, were imitated by the courtiers. These Chinese court dances were in turn copied by entertainers of the Japanese court, who have retained some of them to this day. Even the Tang emperor Xuanzong (reigned 712–56 C.E.) arranged a Central Asian tune for his favorite courtesan, the famous Yang Guifei, to dance to. The dance was called "Rainbow Chemise, Feathered Dress," and the lady, we are told, wore a special costume covered with dazzling golden feathers that had been sent to the emperor as tribute from a far country.[13] Little clay statuettes of musicians and dancers memorialized such musical events and sometimes show us women dancing with tubular sleeves much longer than their arms. Still-earlier representations of sleeve dancing in China come from tombs of the Han dynasty, just after the Silk Road opened (fig. 3.13, fig. 3.14).[14]

3.13 Women with ultralong sleeves depicted dancing: Left, figures on stamped brick found in Sichuan, Eastern Han dynasty, 25–220 C.E. (after Xun Zhou and Chunming Gao, *5000 Years of Chinese Costume* [San Francisco: China Books and Publishers, 1988], fig. 710). Center, pottery figurine found with seven pottery musicians in tomb near Huhechaote, Mongolia, 5th century C.E. (after Adam Kessler, *Empires Beyond the Great Wall* [Los Angeles: Natural History Museum, 1994], fig. 51). Right, porcelain figure now in Shanghai Museum, Tang dynasty, 618–907 C.E. (after Zhou and Gao, *5000 Years of Chinese Costume*, fig. 172)

3.14 A Pair of Painted Pottery Female Dancers, China, Tang dynasty, 618–907; height 25.5 cm. From the Collection of Ruth Stricker; photograph by Maggie Nimkin. The young girls are shown dancing with one arm raised up and the other arm down close to the side, one dancer with both hands covered by her long sleeves and the other with delicate hands showing. See p. 56.

Costumes of this sort still existed all along the Silk Road early in the twentieth century. The Swedish explorer Sven Hedin (1865–1952) photographed Central Asian women wearing very long, skinny sleeves, with the ends and a great deal of sleeve cloth pushed up over the wrists to free the hands for work; and when some of his Tarim workmen and their wives put on a party for him, he sketched the women dancing around the bonfire flapping their long sleeves exactly like the Han and Tang court ladies.[15]

The people whom Hedin recorded were Turkic, but the sleeves were not native to

3.15 Woman's outfit with ultralong sleeves. From South or Central Great Russia, early 20th century. Courtesy of the Rosalie Whyel Museum of Doll Art, Bellevue, Washington. Photograph by Elizabeth Barber

them either. For one thing, it was only near the close of the Tang dynasty that the Tarim Basin and the central Silk Road were taken over by Turkic speakers (namely the Uyghurs, who give their name to the region now). Furthermore, women dancing with such sleeves are already depicted in wall paintings at Turfan in the sixth century C.E. The pre-Turkic inhabitants of these desert basins were largely Iranians and Tokharians, both Indo-European groups who had arrived in the Bronze Age, between roughly 2000 and 500 B.C.E., long before Han soldiers first opened the Silk Road late in the second century B.C.E.. So where had the Central Asians gotten their extended sleeves?

Farther west one can trace several traditions of ultra-long sleeves, for example, among the Slavs. Both peasant and aristocratic women's dress in South and Central Great Russia carried extended—even floor-length—sleeves until the Russian Revolution (fig. 3.15). We can glimpse them, here and there, in drawings all the way back to the eleventh and twelfth centuries C.E., the heyday of Kievan Russia, when we find an especially large number of depictions[16] (fig. 3.16). They occur on metal bracelets preserved in hoards of precious wedding jewelry that the frantic owners hid from marauders and never came back to retrieve. The hinged, tubular bracelets, which ordinarily held the sleeves above the wrists, show scenes of women dancing with hair and sleeves loosened, accompanied by men playing a zither-shaped stringed instrument known as a *gusli*, or psaltery.

Wooden soundboards of several of these early Slavic psaltery have been excavated.[17] In fact, stringed instruments seem to have been greatly favored all across the steppes in early times. The oldest preserved bowed instrument was found in a frozen tomb at Pazyryk in the Altai Mountains (eight hundred kilometers north of the Silk Road), from which also came the phoenix-embroidered silk.[18] Furthermore, a carved stone relief (fig. 3.17) of about 1300 B.C.E. at Alaca Höyük, in Turkey, a major center of the chariot-driving, steppe-related Hittites, contains the earliest depiction of a stringed instrument with a violin-cello-shaped soundboard, held across the musician's body like a guitar, to be strummed.

A magnificent fifteenth-century copy of a lavish thirteenth-century manuscript, the Radziwill Chronicle, not only depicts the sleeve dance but explains it. It was performed

by young women at the summer Rusalii festival, held in honor of female fertility spirits called the *rusalki* or vily ("rose spirits" or "willies"—two regional names for the same thing).[19] The long, white linen sleeves apparently imitated the wings of the white swans and wild geese believed to be the visible forms of the spirit-maidens.

Here at last, then, we find a possible reason for the creation of the sleeve and its dance: a myth-based analogy of white sleeves for white wings.

The Radziwill Chronicle, I should add, also sometimes shows men with long sleeves covering their hands, but only and specifically when they are shown as passive, not active, such as when asleep, bewailing the dead, or being addressed by a king or a saint. Medieval Persian art shows not dissimilar conventions for men with sleeve-covered hands. Presumably the Rusalii dancers, too, were passive, in the sense that they were mere channels to help divine fertility flow into the community.

But before the Slavs lived in Kievan Russia (now Ukraine), Scythians and Sarmatians and other Iranian tribes occupied the area. Iranian tribes, in fact, ranged the length of the steppes for millennia. We have seen them introducing horses, chariots, and new divination methods into northern China in the second millennium B.C.E., and introducing Chinese silk to the Greeks on the shores of the Black Sea in the next millennium. Small surprise, then, that rich women's burials in the Ukrainian steppes reveal considerable evidence for the ultralong sleeve as early as the fourth century B.C.E.

The key features of these burials, which are so rich that the occupants must have been princesses or priestesses or both, are a high headdress, either cylindrical or pointed, covered with repoussé gold foil; a mirror; wide bracelets on each wrist; gold foil platelets that had been sewn all over the clothing; and a shallow bowl of the sort the Greeks used for libations to the gods. Just such a woman is shown on some of the platelets and on one of the gold headdresses—seated in a chair with attendants about her (fig. 3.18). She wears a cylindrical diadem on her head, and over her shoulders a coat with ultralong sleeves, while she holds a mirror for divination in her hand. (Divination with reflective

3.16 Women dancing with ultralong sleeves, and musicians playing the stringed *gusli* or psaltery, Kievan Russia, 12th–13th centuries C.E. The images come mostly from wedding bracelets used to hold up the sleeves, plus one from a chronicle miniature showing a pagan festival. Left to right: from Staryj Rjazan', State Historical Museum, Moscow, Serensk (casting mold), Kiev State Historical Museum (dancer and first player), Radziwill Chronicle, Staryj Rjazan'.

3.17 Musician, from Hittite scene of circuslike entertainers. Stone relief from Alaca Höyük, Turkey, ca. 1300 B.C.E. Note the frets and the viol-shaped soundbox with ten round holes—the earliest known representation of such an instrument. The man wears shoes with turned-up toes like those still worn in southeastern Europe today.

FASHIONED FROM FIBER

3.18 Women (probably priestesses) with extended sleeves and tall diadems holding round mirrors; Scythian, 4th century B.C.E. These images were found on ornaments from rich graves of women clearly dressed and equipped this way, in Zaporozhje and Cherkassy Districts, Ukraine. Left: from gold repoussé dress ornament; right: from gold repoussé diadem (after L. Klochko, "Plechovyj odjag skif'janok," *Arkheologija* 3 (1992): 95–106, figs. 2, 1)

surfaces continues to this day in Eastern Europe, from the Baltic to the Mediterranean, on the dates of the old Rusalii festivals—specifically to answer women's questions about marriage and fertility.)[20]

Evidence from Greece and Crete suggests that the myths and customs that underlie the women's use of the ultralong sleeve may go back further still, for we find bird-girls with extended sleeves depicted in Greece in 700 B.C.E. and in Crete in 1600 B.C.E., along with myths of spirit-maidens that bring fertility and/or turn into birds.[21] Bronze Age Minoans and Classical Greeks, horse-riding Scythian priestesses, Han and Tang court ladies, medieval Slavic brides, and Turkic laborers' wives—all knew of and danced with the ultralong sleeve.

And so today, when we watch a lady in the Chinese opera waving water sleeves of colorful Central Asian silks to the music of stringed instruments, we are in fact watching many thousands of years of cultural influences across Eurasia—traits that have traveled far, metamorphosed much, and meant many things to people along the course of the Silk Road. •

1 See E. J. W. Barber, *Prehistoric Textiles* (Princeton: Princeton University Press, 1991), for discussions of the evidence for those fibers and textiles prior to ca. 400 B.C.E. mentioned in this chapter.

2 Sergei I. Rudenko, *Frozen Tombs of Siberia,* trans. M. W. Thompson (Berkeley: University of California Press, 1970), pp. 174–78, figs. 89–92.

3 Burton Watson, *Records of the Grand Historian of China* (New York: Columbia University Press, 1961), pp. 166, 170, et passim.

4 Victor H. Mair, "Old Sinitiic *mʸag...", *Early China* 15 (1990): 44, reconstructs the Old Chinese form as *sʸəg-. See also Elizabeth W. Barber, *The Mummies of Ürümchi* (New York: W.W. Norton; London: Macmillan, 1999), p. 202.

5 Barber, *Mummies of Ürümchi,* p. 208. See also Samuel Kurinski, *The Glassmakers* (New York: Hippocrene Books, 1991).

6 James Mallory and Victor H. Mair, *The Tarim Mummies* (London: Thames and Hudson, 2000), color pl. IX and cover.

7 Kang Chao, *The Development of Cotton Textile Production in China* (Cambridge: Harvard University Press for East Asian Research Center, 1977), pp. 4–18. For a handy compilation of all the data relating to earliest cotton, see R. A. Jairazbhoy, *Pakistan Gave the World Cotton and Paper* (Lahore: Ferozsons, 1996).

8 For fuller descriptions of this mummy and all the following ones, together with their clothing, see Barber, *Mummies of Ürümchi.*

9 Mair, "Old Sinitiic *mʸag...", discusses all these words, with further references. See also Barber, *Mummies of Ürümchi,* pp. 200–202.

10 See note 9; and see Barber, *Mummies of Ürümchi,* fig. 10.5, for the foreigners in early China.

11 See Elizabeth W. Barber, *Women's Work: The First 20,000 Years* (New York: W.W. Norton, 1994), pp. 127–37.

12 Edward H. Schafer, *The Golden Peaches of Samarkand: A Study of T'ang Exotics* (Berkeley: University of California Press, 1963), is a rich compendium of all the Tang exotica, including costume, music, and dance; see esp. pp. 52–53.

13 Ibid.

14 E. J. W. Barber, "The Curious Tale of the Ultra-long Sleeve: A Eurasian Epic," in *Folk Dress in Europe and Anatolia,* ed. Linda Welters (Oxford and New York: Berg, 1999), discusses Chinese examples on pp. 124–25, and see fig. 7.3d.

15 Lasse Berg and Stig Holmqvist, *I Sven Hedins spår* (Stockholm: Carlssons, 1993), photo p. 194, from 1927; Sven Hedin, *My Life as an Explorer,* trans. Alfhild Huebsch (New York: Boni and Liveright, 1925), sketch on p. 253.

16 Barber, "Curious Tale of the Ultra-long Sleeve," pp. 111–17, figs. 7.1b–c (bracelet figures), 7.1e (Radziwill Chronicle miniature); E. J. W. Barber, "On the Origins of the *vily/rusalki,*" in *Varia on the Indo-European Past,* ed. Miriam R. Dexter and Edgar C. Polomé, *Journal of Indo-European Studies,* monograph 19 (Washington, D.C.: Institute for the Study of Man, 1997), pp. 20–24, figs. 5–10.

17 V. P. Darkevich and A. L. Mongait, "Starorjazanskij klad 1966 goda," *Sovetskaja arkheologija* 2 (1967) 217, fig. 6.

18 Vladimir N. Basilov, "The Scythian Harp and the Kazakh Kobyz: In Search of Historical Connections," in *Foundations of Empire,* ed. Gary Seaman (Los Angeles: Ethnographic Press, University of Southern California, 1992), pp. 77–100.

19 For the ethnographic, literary, and archaeological information available on the vily, see Barber, "On the Origins of the *vily/rusalki.*"

20 For Scythian extended sleeves, see Barber, "Curious Tale of the Ultra-long Sleeve," figs. 7.3a–c. For divination, see Barber, "On the Origins of the *vily/rusalki,*" pp. 19–20, fig. 4.

21 Barber, "Curious Tale of the Ultra-long Sleeve," pp. 27–38, figs. 17–18.

Soon after the year 1200, Japanese artists painted a vision of a celestial realm governed by the Buddha Shakyamuni (fig. 4.1). The red-robed Buddha sits on top of Mount Sumeru, the cosmic mountain at the center of the universe that rises out of the cosmic sea. Three concentric rings around the Buddha display human figures and animals, personifications of the celestial bodies. Drawn closer to the central of these three circles, the viewer is surprised to see images that appear familiar.

FOUR • ASTROLOGY AND A JAPANESE STAR MANDALA ELIZABETH TEN GROTENHUIS

They look like the signs of the western zodiac, and indeed they are.

Here are Leo the lion, Cancer the crab, Taurus the bull, and so on. This eight-hundred-year-old painting is an extraordinary example of the synthesis of astrological knowledge that the ancient Silk Road enabled Asia and the West to share. It is also a picture of a Buddhist realm of enlightenment that evokes early Indian mythology. A pair of serpents, entwining the cosmic mountain on which the Buddha sits, seem to churn the cosmic ocean to create the ambrosia of life and the world in which we

4.1 Star Mandala (*Hoshi mandara*). Japan, Kamakura period, 13th century. Panel: ink, color, and gold on silk; 109.9 x 81.1 cm. Denman Waldo Ross Collection, courtesy Museum of Fine Arts, Boston

live (fig. 4.1a). About the same time that the Japanese picture was being painted, another reworking of this myth was under way in another part of Asia. Architects in Cambodia—as unaware of the Japanese painters as the Japanese painters were of them—were building the temple-city of Angkor Thom, whose ground plan was probably based on the same Indian myth and also on local notions about astrology. In this chapter, I will discuss the Japanese painting, emphasizing the exchange of astrological knowledge from the Mediterranean Sea to the Sea of Japan that resulted in the surprising inclusion of western signs of the zodiac in the painting. I will then return to Angkor Thom, exploring the myth that may inform both the Japanese painting and the ground plan of the Cambodian city. Both examples underscore the complex transfer of culture made possible by the Silk Road, along both its land and sea routes.

THE STAR MANDALA   The Japanese painting, now in the Museum of Fine Arts, Boston, is called a Star Mandala (*hoshi mandara*)[1] (see fig. 4.1). A mandala is a depiction of a realm of enlightenment, a sanctified realm where identification between the human and the sacred occurs. In traditional Buddhist usage, this word usually indicates a circular or square configuration, with a center that radiates outward into compartmentalized areas. The deity at the center of the configuration, who signifies absolute truth, engages in reciprocal interactions with figures in the outer precincts, who signify manifested aspects of that truth. A practitioner, visualizing and meditating on the mandala's peripheral elements, unites these outer manifestations in the center of the mandala and then internally absorbs the mandala as a whole.[2]

Many mandalas—like this Japanese Star Mandala—take the form of two-dimensional images meant to be hung on temple walls as focal points for devotion, contemplation, and rituals. Sometimes they are spread out on altar tops for specific ceremonies, recalling what must have been among the earliest kinds of mandalas made in India—sacred configurations drawn in sand on the ground or on a low platform. The two-dimensional mandalas are, however, meant to be mentally transformed into three-dimensional realms, often palatial structures, during contemplation and ritual. Figure 4.2 shows the Star Mandala as it might be envisioned in a three-dimensional construction. In their two-dimensional forms, these mandalas often look like architectural ground plans, seen from an aerial viewpoint.

In the Japanese Star Mandala, we can imagine the Buddha Shakyamuni sitting on top of Mount Sumeru, which rises through a three-tiered circular universe below. This is Shakyamuni of the Golden Wheel, a glorified form of the

4.2 Star mandala envisioned as a three-dimensional realm. Drawing by Linda Z. Ardrey

4.1a Detail, Star Mandala—central section

74

historical Buddha, so named because of the golden wheel he holds in his hands as he sits in meditation on a lotus throne on the cosmic mountain. (Wheels also appear at the edge of the halo behind the body of the Buddha.) The wheel signifies the Buddhist teachings that the historical Buddha set in motion circling through time and space after he attained enlightenment in about 450 B.C.E. Enlightenment is an ineffable state of profound wisdom, boundless compassion, and joyous tranquility whose attainment frees the practitioner from bondage to the cycle of birth and death and rebirth. Contemplation and veneration of mandalas are believed to help practitioners approach and experience the enlightened state. The representation of Shakyamuni, shown here in monastic robes, recalls the historical Buddha who was thought to have worn such garb when he lived and taught in northern India (see fig. 4.1a). He is also furnished with the characteristic signs of a Buddha or "Enlightened One." These signs include the close-shorn hair and a protuberance signifying wisdom on top of the head; a hair tuft, again signifying wisdom, in the middle of the forehead; elongated earlobes recalling the holes created by the heavy earrings that the historical Buddha wore during his early princely life; and three rings at his neck recalling the three rings of the conch shell, which is blown during religious rituals.[3]

By the time this painting was rendered in thirteenth-century Japan, the religion of Buddhism had undergone many transformations. In the Mahayana (Greater Vehicle) tradition that spread through Asia from about the beginning of the first century, Shakyamuni came to be seen as one of many Buddhas who are assisted in their activities of salvation by sacred figures called bodhisattvas, literally, "enlightenment beings" or "beings intent on enlightenment." Bodhisattvas are inherently enlightened beings who postpone their own complete emancipation from the world in order to save all sentient creatures. Mahayana Buddhism continued to evolve, finding expression in a number of different sects and movements. Its last major development, a highly complex form of belief and practice articulated by the seventh century, can be loosely termed Esoteric Buddhism. Mandalas like the Japanese Star Mandala play an important role in rituals and practices of this later form of Buddhism.

On the circular platform closest to the central Buddha appear sixteen figures. Above Shakyamuni are personifications of the seven stars of the Big Dipper or Great Dipper, the group of seven principal stars in the constellation of Ursa Major (the Great Bear) in the northern hemisphere.[4] Each figure appears in the center of a white disk that recalls the moon but that, if the mandala is envisioned as a three-dimensional realm, also provides a circular seat on which the deity can sit. All the personified stars are shown in Chinese dress, reflecting Chinese influence in the synthesis of astrological knowledge, from both West and East Asia.

Below Shakyamuni are personifications of the nine planetoids, often called the nine luminaries. These are the Sun, the Moon, two (invisible) lunar nodes, and the five planets of traditional visual astronomy that appear to the naked eye as bright stars—Mercury, Venus, Mars, Jupiter, and Saturn. (The other three planets, besides Earth, that revolve around the Sun—Uranus, Neptune, and Pluto—were discovered fairly recently. Uranus, near the limit of visibility, was discovered in 1781; Neptune, somewhat fainter, in 1846; and Pluto, so faint it was detected on long-exposure photographs only with a powerful telescope, in 1930.) Believing that the Earth was the fixed center of the universe, the ancients called the Sun, the Moon, and the five planets, which seemed to them to move around Earth, the "wandering bodies." ("Planet" is from a Greek word meaning "wanderer.") They distinguished these wandering bodies from the stars, which they saw as fixed. The two lunar nodes, given the names Rahu and Ketu in Sanskrit, were invisible phenomena postulated by Indian astrologers to exist at the nodes of the Moon's orbit, to account for eclipses.

The twelve signs of the zodiac appear in the middle concentric circle of deities. The zodiac (from the Greek *zodiakos kuklos,* "circle of animals") is an imaginary celestial belt, sixteen degrees wide, that includes the paths of the Sun, the Moon, and the principal planets. The middle line of the zodiac is the ecliptic, the apparent orbital course of the Sun as seen from what was believed to be the unmoving position of Earth. (The apparent path of the Sun through a year is, we know now, actually Earth's orbit around the Sun.) The zodiac is divided into twelve zones, or constellations, each thirty degrees in size and each designated by a sign. Most of the signs in the Museum of Fine Arts painting are represented in accordance with the signs familiar to students of Western astrology, although in some cases they are Indianized (the vase of Aquarius) or Sinicized (Virgo and Gemini, here ethnically Chinese). Leo the lion is above the head of Shakyamuni. Continuing in a clockwise direction around this belt, the viewer discovers Gemini the twins; Libra the balance; Scorpio the scorpion (fig. 4.1b); Sagittarius the archer (fig. 4.1b); Capricornus the goat (who is often a half-goat and half-fish and is shown here as a sea monster); Aquarius the water carrier; Pisces the fishes; Aries the ram (fig. 4.1c); Taurus the bull (fig. 4.1c); Virgo the virgin; and, finally, at the conclusion of the circle, Cancer the crab. Each of these signs is found in the middle of a white halo, like the individual stars of the Big Dipper.

Westerners may be surprised to find in the Japanese Star Mandala Asian versions of the figures that stare at them in newspaper horoscopes. In fact, this Star Mandala, although painted in Japan in the early thirteenth century, reflects the Tang dynasty (618–907), when the Western zodiac was in use in China. Soon after the Tang dynasty, the Chinese rejected the Western zodiac for their own, pre-Tang, animal representations

of the zodiac. The zodiac commemorating the following cycle of twelve animals is still used throughout East Asia: mouse, ox, tiger, hare, dragon,

4.1b Detail, Star Mandala—
right side

snake, horse, sheep, monkey, cock, dog, boar. The Japanese Star Mandala, although
painted much later than the Tang dynasty, was obviously modeled on iconographic
drawings or paintings that had entered Japan during the Tang dynasty or that reflected
the Tang conception of the heavens.

The outer concentric circle of the Star Mandala shows twenty-eight deities, each
representing a stage or constellation along the Moon's path in the zodiac. The ancients
knew that it took one month for the Moon to complete the cycle from new Moon to
full Moon to new Moon again. Although the lunar month involves either a twenty-
nine- or thirty-day cycle, these twenty-eight constellations were generally thought to
relate to the Moon as it changed shape from day to day.

ASTROLOGY   Astrology, which for the ancients was synonymous with astronomy, is
the art of predicting the fate of human beings and of the world at large from indications
given by celestial bodies. Astrologers were among the first scientists. Believing that the
order of the stars reflected a universal order, astrologers were eager to harness that order
for the benefit of humankind. This search for order seems to have absorbed human
beings from a very early time. Twenty-five thousand years ago, humans cut notches in
reindeer bones and mammoth tusks that may be records of the cycles of the Moon.

Astrology originated in Mesopotamia, perhaps as early as the third millennium
B.C.E. It was natural to look to the celestial bodies for clues to human destiny because it
was easy to observe the influence of the Sun on Earth and the Moon on the seas. Why
shouldn't the celestial bodies influence humans as well? Imagining Earth as the unmoving center of the universe, astrologers studied the planets, which seemed to approach
and recede, move above and below, behind and in front of the fixed stars. It seemed log-
ical that such powerful and active celestial bodies might very well be instrumental in
governing human activities and destinies on Earth.

The study of astrology was highly developed by the ancient Babylonians, who, for
example, around 450 B.C.E. perfected the theory of the great belt of the zodiac divided
among twelve constellations or signs. The concept of the zodiac had first been suggested
even earlier, in Chaldea (612–539 B.C.E.). The origin and identification of the constellations of the zodiac remain, however, quite mysterious. The number twelve obviously
refers to the number of Moon cycles in a year, a system of counting that probably began
as a way of measuring time. But we do not know how the twelve divisions came to be
identified with specific creatures or objects. Only two of the zodiacal signs are easily
associated with actual stars in the sky. One is Scorpio the scorpion (see fig. 4.1b),

associated with a grouping of fifteen stars that (with a little imagination) calls to mind the stinging tail of that dangerous insect, prevalent in West Asia. The other is Gemini the twins, the sign associated with two principal stars (Castor and Pollux) that shine with approximately the same intensity.

CHINA Chinese astronomy/astrology had probably begun to receive influences from the Babylonians by the sixth century B.C.E. at the latest.[5] Astrological studies spread from Mesopotamia to Greece about the middle of the fourth century B.C.E. and reached Rome before the Christian era. Egyptian, Indian, and Chinese astrology and astronomy reflect Greek as well as Mesopotamian ideas, although the Chinese added their own theories, such as Daoist concepts about yang and yin (male and female principles) to what they had absorbed from the West along the Silk Road.[6] Yang and yin energies are embodied, for example, in the representations of the Sun and the Moon in the Star Mandala. The Sun is depicted as a male deity holding a circular red sphere who drives three horses (see fig. 4.1c). This figure recalls the Sun deity, Surya, from India and also represents the yang, the male, active principle associated with birth, spring, brightness, the day. Conversely, the Moon in this mandala is embodied in the form of a woman holding a mirror that reflects light, just as the Moon reflects light (see fig. 4.1b). This figure represents the yin, the female, passive principle associated with death, autumn, darkness, the night.

The Japanese Star Mandala recalls a dynamic period for astrological studies in China—the Tang dynasty, when astrologers and astronomers from many lands worked in the capital of Chang'an (now Xi'an) furthering their studies and competing for imperial favor. Many texts on astrology were disseminated in Tang China. Some even attained scriptural classification: the standard modern edition of the Chinese Buddhist canon in the section on Esoteric Buddhist teachings includes fourteen Tang texts on astrology. Esoteric Buddhists, who believed the world could and should be manipulated by proper magico-spiritual means, were particularly interested in understanding the influences of the planets and the stars on human events. Many Esoteric masters were involved in calendar making and in other astrological studies, a world of intellectual endeavor strictly regulated and forbidden to all but a chosen few.

4.1c Detail, Star Mandala—left side. Note the celestial body personified as a woman playing the lute (Chinese: *pipa*; Japanese: *biwa*) below and slightly to the right of the personified Sun.

Although much of Tang astrology was ultimately indebted to ancient Mesopotamian and Greek studies, the Chinese saw the heavenly bodies through an Indian lens. In eighth-century China, three Indian families— the Kasyapa, Gautama, and Kumara—exerted a virtual monopoly on the important official calendrical calculations. The most eminent of these Indian astrologers, named, like the historical Buddha, Gautama Siddhartha,

was the director of the royal observatory and was called "the Astronomer Royal." He translated the *Nine Planets (Luminaries) Almanac* from Sanskrit into Chinese in 718. This Greco-Indian work was known for its excellent prediction of eclipses. Gautama also taught the Chinese more exact methods of predicting solar and lunar eclipses. Other influential Indians in China in the eighth century were the Esoteric masters Subhakarasimha, who was involved in calendar reform, and Amoghavajra, who was also associated with Indian-style calendar computation and who translated into Chinese astrological texts, which were written from a Buddhist point of view.[7]

JAPAN   Chinese astrology entered Japan as part of the wholesale importation of continental culture from the sixth century onward. The Star Mandala, in the circular form seen here, was envisioned by the Tendai abbot Keien (949–1019). A rectangular Star Mandala, in which the same personified celestial bodies appear, but in different locations in rectangular rather than circular courts, was devised by the Shingon abbot Kanjo of Ninnaji (died 1125). The oldest extant Star Mandala in the circular format is the mid-twelfth-century painting from the Buddhist temple Horyuji near Nara.[8] The oldest extant Star Mandala in the rectangular format is the mid-twelfth-century painting from the Buddhist temple Kumedadera in Osaka.[9] The Museum of Fine Arts, Boston, also owns a rectangular Star Mandala dated to the eighteenth or nineteenth century[10] (fig. 4.3). This painting is in such a good state of preservation that it allows us to see clearly the various figures in a Star Mandala.

These star mandalas first appeared in Japan during the Heian period (794–1185), when astrology, star worship, and divination were much in vogue. The mandalas were the main objects of devotion in the Big Dipper rite, which was conducted to prolong life and to avoid the calamities of droughts, earthquakes, pestilence, war, and floods. By making offerings to the constellations that presided over destiny, devotees hoped to avoid both personal and national disaster. It is significant that the Star Mandala is also called the Big Dipper Mandala, because at this period the Japanese believed that the star

4.3 Star Mandala (*Hoshi mandara*). Japan, Edo period, 18th–19th century. Unmounted painting: ink, color, and gold on silk; 83 x 51.9 cm. William Sturgis Bigelow Collection, courtesy Museum of Fine Arts, Boston. An unusual feature of this mandala is the pair of Buddha-like heads on the serpents wound around the base of the cosmic mountain. In earlier star mandalas (see fig. 4.1), the heads of the serpents appear more cobra-like.

that most affected an individual's fate was the one of the seven stars of the Big Dipper associated with his or her year of birth. Sometimes, when it was thought that an unlucky star had obstructed the main star, a practitioner would set up an altar and make offerings to the main auspicious star. Also in accordance with the year of birth, a devotee was associated with one of the nine luminaries. Ceremonies meant to circumvent misfortune were sometimes performed in front of altars with representations of both the main (Big Dipper) star and the associated celestial body from the nine luminaries.

Wound around the base of the cosmic mountain in the Japanese star mandalas are two human-headed serpents (see figs. 4.1a, 4.3). The two serpents, often disregarded in writings on star mandalas, probably reflect an ancient Indian myth. The story is usually associated with Hindu mythology, but it makes its way into Buddhist lore as well and, as we will see in a moment, may even shape the layout of cities. The two serpents subtly recall the myth of the churning of the Ocean of Milk, in which Earth emerges in the form of a goddess along with many other beneficent deities and objects as two powerful forces struggle to obtain the elixir of immortality.[11] Because the celestial beings, or "gods," (Sanskrit *deva*) are losing battles with their traditional enemies, the antigods (Sanskrit *asura*), the gods devise a plan to defeat the antigods. They entreat Bali, the king of the antigods, to declare a truce and to order his forces to cooperate with the gods in churning the elixir of immortality from the cosmic Ocean of Milk. The gods promise to share the elixir with the antigods, but, of course, have no intention of doing so. If the gods can obtain and drink the elixir, they will be able to defeat the antigods for all time.

The antigods agree to the plan, and the gods approach the great Hindu deity Vishnu and ask for his help. Thanks to the intervention of Vishnu, the so-called king of mountains, Mount Mandara, is moved from its location to the east of Mount Sumeru, the home of the gods and the center of the universe, to be used as the churning dasher. Then the multiheaded king of serpents, Vasuki, is enticed from the bottom of the Ocean of Milk to serve as the churning cord. Vishnu supports Mount Mandara in his incarnation as the tortoise Kurma, while the gods and antigods wrap the serpent around the mountain and take their positions—the gods near the tail of the serpent, the antigods near the head (see fig. 4.9).

The churning proceeds energetically, and eventually various treasures, including Earth in the form of a goddess as well as the long-coveted elixir of immortality, emerge from the ocean. When the antigods discover that they are not to be included in the sharing of the elixir they begin to wage war against the gods. Vishnu intervenes, helps the gods to win, but, in order to safeguard the potion, he leaves with the elixir before the gods can drink it.

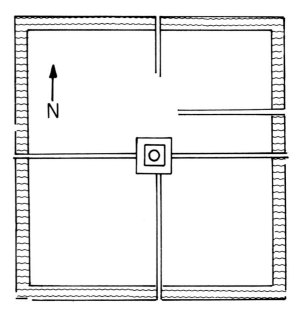

4.4 Groundplan of Angkor Thom. Drawing by Linda Z. Ardrey

CAMBODIA   In the year 1200, the Khmer king Jayavarman VII was building the city of Angkor Thom at the Angkor complex in Cambodia. Unlike his predecessors, who had been Hindu, Jayavarman VII was a Buddhist ruler, and he laid out his magnificent temple-city, with its many Buddhist sanctuaries, to glorify the Buddha. He placed at the center of the city a temple dedicated not to Vishnu or the other important Hindu deity Shiva, but rather to the Buddha. And it is possible to see the ground plan of the city of Angkor Thom as a symbolic allusion to the churning of the Ocean of Milk[12] (fig. 4.4).

The ground plan of Angkor Thom also resembles a mandala; like a mandala, it is a kind of cosmic map, laying out a sacred realm in microcosm, showing the relations among the various powers active in that realm, and offering devotees a precinct where enlightenment can take place. The Buddha is venerated in the very center of the city in his temple called the Bayon (fig. 4.5). Some fifty towers rise up around this central sanctuary with colossal faces at each of the four sides of each of the towers, gazing protectively in all directions (fig. 4.6).

4.5 The Bayon at Angkor Thom, Cambodia—view from east, ca. 1200. Courtesy ACSAA color slide project, University of Michigan, Ann Arbor

ASTROLOGY AND A JAPANESE STAR MANDALA

The city has a quadrilateral ground plan, over three kilometers on a side, with a city wall eight meters high. It is surrounded by a moat one hundred meters wide, with bridges over the moat at five places. There is one bridge at each of the cardinal axes (north, south, east, and west) and a fifth bridge on the eastern face, leading to the palace in the north-central part of the city. The balustrades of the bridges seem to have been ornamented with a row of fifty-four figures on each side, each row of figures holding the body of a giant serpent. Although most of the bridges are now in disrepair, the south bridge has been restored to show the original conception. We can, therefore, imagine the overall ground plan, marveling at the vision of Jayavarman VII.

By the time Angkor Thom was completed in the early thirteenth century, the five bridges probably presented 540 balustrade figures holding serpents' bodies. On each of the bridges, one balustrade featured the gods and the other balustrade the antigods. The myth of the churning of the Ocean of Milk was brilliantly miniaturized in this city plan, where the cosmic mountain that was used as the churning dasher was symbolized by the circular temple that actually existed in the city center. This temple was conceived as a temple-mountain identical to Mount Sumeru that rises through the center of the Buddhist (and Hindu) universes. Here the Mount Mandara of the original myth becomes conflated with Mount Sumeru (also called Mount Meru). The churning of the cosmic mountain can be imagined as taking place on the north-south and east-west axes of the city, along the bridges and avenues that led to the central

4.6 Detail of a face on one of the towers of the Bayon, Angkor Thom. Cambodia, late 12th century, stone. Freer Gallery of Art Photograph Reference Collection, Freer Gallery of Art and Arthur M. Sackler Gallery Archives, Smithsonian Institution, Washington, D.C.

4.7 View of restored south bridge at Angkor Thom, 1995, showing a team of gods (at left, the western side) and a team of antigods (at right, the eastern side) holding serpents to form the bridge balustrades. Courtesy of Eleanor Mannikka

ASTROLOGY AND A JAPANESE STAR MANDALA

temple-mountain. The cosmic ocean that was being churned was represented by the grand moat surrounding the city. Teams of fifty-four gods and antigods on the north bridge battled with teams of fifty-four antigods and gods on the south bridge. The same disposition occurred on the eastern and western bridges. Each team of gods and antigods held a giant serpent appearing only on the balustrade but which could be imagined as winding around the cosmic mountain (fig. 4.7). In this hypothesis, the Angkor Thom architects were freely interpreting the myth, which suggested that a group of gods and a group of antigods were churning with a single serpent, one team near the head of the serpent, one near its tail. At Angkor Thom, in fact, four giant serpents may be imagined as circling the cosmic mountain, teams of gods with their own serpents jockeying with teams of antigods with their own serpents on both the north-south and east-west avenues. Figure 4.8 shows the massive head of a god from one of the balustrades at Angkor Thom.

The Angkor Thom ground plan not only suggests the myth of the churning of the Cosmic Ocean, but it also may have astrological implications. Like the Japanese Star Mandala, which shows a synthesis of astrological knowledge from both West and East, Angkor Thom may show a synthesis of the Indian myth with notions about the movement of the celestial bodies that are peculiarly Khmer. The significance of the number fifty-four is Khmer in origin, and by combining the myth with the fifty-four–fifty-four pairing, a unique interpretation of the roles played by the Sun and the Moon in the cosmos becomes possible. Once more we see evidence of that extraordinary synthesis of knowledge that occurred along the historical Silk Road.

As Eleanor Mannikka points out, the Khmers were the only people in South and Southeast Asia to enumerate exactly fifty-four gods and fifty-four antigods in the churning myth.[13] They depicted these figures often, not only on the bridges at Angkor Thom but also as low-relief carvings, for example, at the twelfth-century Hindu temple-city of Angkor Wat (fig. 4.9). The sum of these numbers, 108, is another number that is exceptionally important in both Hindu and Buddhist lore: Vishnu has 108 names; Buddhists

4.8 Head of a Deva (god). Cambodia, Angkor Thom, late 12th–early 13th century. Sandstone, height approx. 80 cm. Alice and Helen Coburn Fund, courtesy Museum of Fine Arts, Boston, © 2001

must overcome 108 deficiencies; there are 108 beads found on both Hindu and Buddhist prayer beads.

Various representations of the churning myth in different parts of Asia show the Sun and the Moon close to the cosmic mountain being churned by the gods and the antigods. This is true in the Japanese Star Mandala, where the personified Sun appears on the left side of the painting near the cosmic mountain (see fig. 4.1c) and the personified Moon appears on the right (see fig. 4.1b). Significantly, the Sun and the Moon move approximately fifty-four degrees north and south during the year. Mannikka goes on to explain:

> On the day of the winter solstice, around December 22, the sun is at its southernmost position in the sky. The sun starts to move northward with each successive sunrise until, on June 21, the summer solstice day, it is at its northernmost point in the sky. After that, it starts to rise farther south each day. This north-south and south-north solar oscillation ranges between 49 degrees 12 minutes and 43 degrees 58 minutes,

4.9 Churning of the Ocean of Milk by gods and antigods at Angkor Wat, third gallery, east side, south half. Cambodia, first half 12th century. Courtesy ACSAA color slide project, University of Michigan, Ann Arbor. The gods appear to the right and the antigods to the left, from the viewer's perspective.

depending on the year in question. Could the venerated numbers 49 and 44 derive from the limits of the sun's yearly oscillation? The moon oscillates between north-south extremes across the celestial equator in an arc that can reach a maximum of 59 degrees 28 minutes. Could the 54/54 pairing at Angkor also trace its origins to solar and lunar movement? Although there is no precise and unvarying figure for the amount of north-south arc crossed by the sun and moon, the average degree of *maximum* oscillation is 54 degrees 20 minutes for both the sun and moon combined, or 108 degrees for the annual north-south, back and forth, movement. At present the sun oscillates at 46 degrees 54 minutes, and the arc is decreasing. The 54 degree maximum average arc may have inspired the 54/54 pairing of gods and antigods in Cambodia."[14]

The casual observer of a Japanese Star Mandala and the casual visitor to Angkor Thom can be pardoned for overlooking the subtle but important connections between the two works.[15] The painting hangs mutely on a wall, looking to the uninitiated more like a bull's-eye for archery practice than like celestial regions meant to be imagined as a grand three-dimensional realm. Angkor Thom overwhelms the visitor with the remains of its stone temples and stone images. And yet, Indian mythology lies at the heart of both painting and city. Added to this are complex interpretations of the movement of heavenly bodies. In the case of the Star Mandala, astrological conceptions from Babylonia—including the Western signs of the zodiac—intermingle with Indian and Chinese notions about the universe. In the case of Angkor Thom, Indian mythology meshes with indigenous Cambodian conceptions about the movement of the Sun and the Moon through a year. The Japanese Star Mandala and the city of Angkor Thom are but two of countless examples showing related kinds of cross-cultural syntheses as ideas traveled the ancient Silk Road on land and water routes from the Mediterranean Sea to the Pacific Ocean. •

1   This painting is reproduced in black and white in Museum of Fine Arts, Boston, *Bosuton bijutsukan Nihon bijutsu chôsa zuroku* (Pictorial record and investigation of Japanese art in the Museum of Fine Arts, Boston), 2 vols. (Boston: Museum of Fine Arts; Tokyo: Kodansha, 1997), p. 122, fig. 16 (pictorial record); p. 7, no. 16 (explanatory notes). This is the first time the painting has been reproduced in color. Thanks to Anne Nishimura Morse, curator of Japanese art, and Masaru Shima, research assistant, Museum of Fine Arts, Boston, for their assistance in expediting new color photography of this painting.

2   For further discussion, see Elizabeth ten Grotenhuis, *Japanese Mandalas: Representations of Sacred Geography* (Honolulu: University of Hawai'i Press, 1999), esp. pp. 1–11.

3   An accessible introduction to Buddhist art is Robert E. Fisher, *Buddhist Art and Architecture* (London: Thames and Hudson, 1993).

4   For discussion of star mandalas and further bibliography, see ten Grotenhuis, *Japanese Mandalas*, pp. 116–21. This Star Mandala is also often called a "Big Dipper (Japanese: *hokuto*) Mandala."

5   Edward H. Schafer, *Pacing the Void: T'ang Approaches to the Stars* (Berkeley: University of California Press, 1977), pp. 10–11.

6   Ibid., p. 3. See also Edward H. Schafer, *The Golden Peaches of Samarkand: A Study of T'ang Exotics* (Berkeley: University of California Press, 1963), pp. 275–76.

7   See also John M. Rosenfield and Elizabeth ten Grotenhuis, *Journey of the Three Jewels: Japanese Buddhist Paintings from Western Collections* (New York: Asia Society, 1979), pp. 106–8.

8   This Star Mandala is reproduced and discussed in English in various sources including ten Grotenhuis, *Japanese Mandalas,* figs. 73–75; Bunsaku Kurata and W. Chie Ishibashi, *Hôryûji: Temple of the Exalted Law* (New York: Japan Society, 1981), no. 29; and Shigeru Nakayama, *A History of Japanese Astronomy: Chinese Background and Western Impact* (Cambridge, Mass.: Harvard University Press, 1969), pp. 205–6.

9   This Star Mandala is reproduced and discussed in English in ten Grotenhuis, *Japanese Mandalas,* fig. 76.

10 This painting is reproduced in black and white in Museum of Fine Arts, Boston, *Bosuton bijutsukan Nihon bijutsu chôsa zuroku,* p. 161, fig. 169 (pictorial record); p. 24, no. 169 (explanatory notes).

11 A recent discussion of this myth is found in Eleanor Mannikka, *Angkor Wat: Time, Space, and Kinship* (Honolulu: University of Hawai'i Press, 1996), pp. 32–33.

12 See, for example, Philip Rawson, *The Art of Southeast Asia* (London: Thames and Hudson, 1967), pp. 98–115. See also Bernard Philippe Groslier, *The Art of Indochina,* trans. George Lawrence (New York: Crown Publishers, 1962), pp. 168–187.

13 Mannikka's argument of the fifty-four–fifty-four pairing is found in her *Angkor Wat,* pp. 33–43.

14 Ibid., pp. 34–36. I also thank Eleanor Mannikka for reading my pages on Angkor Thom and offering valuable suggestions.

15 In recent years Jean Boisselier has presented an alternate hypothesis to explain the ground plan of Angkor Thom. He suggests that the city represents the capital of the deity Indra. Indra's capital was located on the summit of Mount Sumeru and was guarded by serpents, so even in this hypothesis, we see a similarity between the ground plan of Angkor Thom and the Japanese Star Mandala with its central Mount Sumeru encircled by serpents. For further discussion, see Helen Ibbitson Jessup and Thierry Zephir, eds. *Sculpture of Angkor and Ancient Cambodia: Millennium of Glory* (Washington, D.C.: National Gallery of Art, 1997), pp. 117–120.

Kenro Izu has been drawn to sacred sites since his trip to Egypt in 1979 to see and photograph the Pyramids. Izu finds that the world's sacred sites have a spiritual resonance, an atmosphere charged by worshipful attention over millennia. He seeks to convey this aura in his images. On two trips in 1999 and 2000, Izu photographed sacred sites along the roads and byways of the Silk Road. He often traveled the routes that pilgrims, monks, and merchants crossed for centuries. When roads permitted, Izu proceeded by jeep, but he also loaded equipment onto horses, donkeys, or yaks and

walked for days to reach sacred sites located in the deserts of China or the mountains of Tibet and Ladakh, India.

In contrast to many modern photographers who take scores of shots on a single outing, Izu chooses each view and shoots each image only after very careful consideration. Because of the size of the large format negatives (these measure 14 x 20 inches [35.56 x 50.8 cm], the same size as the final prints), he takes only eighty plates on trips that average a month in length. And since Izu typically makes two exposures of each view, he has only forty opportunities to capture the spiritual essence of the sites he encounters. Yet Izu finds that the process is not a limitation, but rather a means for the expression of an intensely focused aesthetic project.

Izu's experience photographing Lamayuru Monastery illustrates his working method and artistic goals (see fig. 5.6).

Text by
DEBRA DIAMOND

One morning in 1999, Izu and his guide reached a mountain road above the Lamayuru Monastery in Ladakh. After unloading his equipment and setting up a large-format camera, a process that takes a full half-hour, Izu began his wait for conditions that would bring out the monastery's spiritual essence. Finally, ten minutes before sundown, a golden light fell upon its stone buildings and the surrounding valley was cast into deep shadow. It was only at this moment that Izu photographed the monastery. In his composition, light and shadow create wedge-shaped masses of grays and blacks that emphasize the rugged and inhospitable immensity of the mountainous landscape. At its center, the gentle sprawl of the monastery radiates with an almost ethereal luminescence, creating an otherworldly effect of peace.

Izu finds his inspiration not only within the spiritual aura of sites, but also in the work of photographers like Samuel Bourne (1834–1912). In the nineteenth century, pioneers of early photography traveled from Europe to Asia to document its topography and monuments. Like those photographers, Izu uses a large-format view camera, which can produce images of startling detail and clarity. In his preference for the platinum print, Izu reveals another affinity with nineteenth-century photographers. Platinum prints are made with a process that uses platinum salts instead of silver salts. For the process, a negative——which must be the same size as the desired image——is exposed to light and contact-printed onto paper coated with a light-sensitive solution of platinum chloride and ferrous salts. The ferric oxalate in the solution reacts with ultraviolet light to reduce the platinum particles out of the solution and into the fibers of the paper. This process creates a photograph with a subtle depth and a matte surface that unifies tones and surface in a manner quite unlike that of the silver print in which the image remains within an emulsion layer atop the paper's surface. Platinum prints are particularly valued for their almost unlimited range of gray tones. Izu exploits the platinum print's potential for middle tones and its delicate surface in such photographs as *Dunhuang Caves, China* (see fig. 5.9). The photograph's subtly modulated tones seem to suggest the centuries of sandstorms that eroded the cliff face into which Buddhist caves were hewn long ago.

Izu's photograph of the Buddhist caves at Dunhuang ignores their brilliantly painted interiors to concentrate upon the mouths of a few caves set within a crumbling cliff wall. When we consider that the mountainside there is honeycombed with almost five hundred caves, we realize that Izu is more interested in capturing the spiritual aura of a site than in documenting its totality as an architectural monument. Often choosing a view of a monument's margins, Izu focuses on the site's relationship to the landscape in order to explore its resonant atmosphere. On his most recent trip to Tibet, Izu had a profound experience that has committed him even further to the exploration of nature's spiritual power. To photograph Mount Kailash, the eternally snow-clad peak sacred to Buddhists, Hindus, and Jains, Izu traveled for six days in a jeep along a bumpy road (see fig. 5.3). Upon reaching the pilgrimage route that circles the mountain's base and transferring his equipment onto a yak, Izu began his search for the ideal vantage point from which to photograph the peak. On the frigid morning of the third day, Izu woke before dawn and set up his camera. Snow had fallen the night before, and a fierce wind had arisen. When dawn came, a shaft of sunlight fell upon the mountain and illuminated the snow gusting about its peak. Izu took one of his typically long exposures. When the exposure was complete, the wind had died down causing the snow to settle, and the rising sun's light illuminated the valley in which Izu was standing. It was too late to produce another image. Izu considers the image of Kailash to convey the essence of his project, the evocation of the sacred resonance of sites worshiped over millennia.

Izu was born in Osaka, Japan, in 1949. He started photographing as a tool for documenting specimens of a medical nature in high school, as it was his dream to become a doctor. In 1968 he entered Nihon University, College of Art, Tokyo, where he formally studied photography. After a brief visit to New York City in 1970, Izu decided to reside permanently there. In 1983, he began to use the platinum technique of printmaking with a custom-made 14 x 20 inch camera. Says Kenro Izu: "Over my 22-year enchantment with stone monuments, I have made photographs in Egypt, Syria, Jordan, Mexico, Chile [Easter Island], England, Scotland, France, Burma, Vietnam, Indonesia, Cambodia, China, India, and Tibet. To capture the spirituality I feel in stone remains and the density of atmosphere that embraces them, I can think of no other medium than platinum prints made by contact printing with large format negatives."[1]

NOTE

Photographs by Kenro Izu published by permission of Kenro Izu.

1   Kenro Izu, *Light over Ancient Angkor: Platinum Prints* (New York: Friends Without A Border, 1996), p. 13.

5.1 **Chuku Monastery, Tibet**

A flat riverbed of the sort that pilgrims follow
on their pilgrimages around Mount Kailash
cuts a swath between the sacred peak and
Chuku Monastery. In this, as in so many of
Izu's Silk Road photographs, the curving path
invites us to enter the landscape and recall the
monks and pilgrims who worshiped and continue to worship there. Within the Buddhist
complex, a mirror angled beneath a skylight
catches the reflection of the mountain and
brings its radiant presence into Chuku's
interior (2000).

5.2 **Tholing Monastery, Tibet**

In the Tibetan tradition, *chortens*, or stupas,
are symbols of the Buddha's continuing imma-
nence as well as representations of his mind
and body. The structures are often erected over
the relics of great monks and enlightened
beings. In the eleventh century, four *chortens*
were constructed in the arid landscape of
Tholing, a monastic complex in western Tibet.
Today only two survive. According to tradition, the remains of the great scholar-monk
Rinchen Zangpo are buried beneath the
northwest *chortens* (2000).

5.3 **Mount Kailash, Tibet**

Izu focuses his composition on the snow-clad peak of Mount Kailash, the Himalayan mountain sacred to Buddhists, Hindus, and Jains. By exploiting a tonal range that extends from jet black to brilliant white, Izu creates a remarkable effect of luminosity and captures the dazzling radiance of Kailash.

Small stones piled up by devotees to commemorate their pilgrimages around the sacred mountain are visible in the darkened foreground. The markers are known as *mani* (jewel) stones, after the most popular mantra of Tibetan Buddhism, *om mani padme hum* (the jewel is in the lotus) (2000).

5.4 Guge, Tibet

Hewn into living rock, Buddhist ritual chambers and monastic cells allowed devotees to turn inward and contemplate the nature of being. In contrast, Izu's panoramic composition invites the viewer to contemplate the caves as moments within an immense landscape.

Izu's image conjures nature's magnificence as a metaphor for the sublime awareness achieved through meditation and worship. In spite of the mountain's complex worked and textured surface, the descending diagonal thrust of its massive form opens effortlessly onto a riverine plain that extends to a luminous far horizon (2000).

98

5.5 **Drepung Monastery, Tibet**

As signs of devotion, pilgrims and monks place prayer flags printed with prayers by sacred sites. In this composition, prayer flags worn fragile by time adorn a shrub by a small *chorten,* or stupa, on a promontory above Drepung Monastery outside Lhasa, Tibet.

Izu draws an implicit connection between small gestures of human devotion and the grandeur of nature. The image's even, high focus and modulated tones unify the intricate details of tattered prayer flags, bristly vegetation, and pitted boulders with a vast sweep of cloud-filled sky (1999).

SACRED SITES ALONG THE SILK ROAD

5.6 **Lamayuru Monastery, Ladakh**

Buddhist monasteries in the Himalayas were not only sites of great sacred power and learning; they were also political entities wielding secular power. Less than two hundred years after its founding in the eleventh century, Lamayuru monks competed with a rival monastic order for the favor of the Mongol overlords in an attempt to gain political power.

The formal qualities of Izu's photograph emphasize the spiritual resonance of Lamayuru Monastery rather than its historical engagements with political power. Passages of light and shadow create a tightly structured composition in which a shaft of piercing sunlight perfectly illuminates the monastery's clustered structures (1999).

5.7 **Hemis Monastery, Ladakh**

Izu often focuses upon the periphery of sacred
sites; these eroding stupas are located just outside the rectangular courtyard of Hemis
Monastery in Ladakh. While the Silk Road
is most often conceptualized as a vast
highway linking China with India and the
Mediterranean, its auxiliary byways played
a crucial role in the transmission of religion,
culture, people, and goods. Located within
northwest India, Ladakh was linked to the
Silk Road through Kashmir and northern
mountain passes but was at various times
part of the Tibetan cultural sphere (1999).

5.8 **Shey Monastery, Ladakh**

These stupas near Shey monastery in Ladakh, India, bear representations of stairways upon their superstructures. The stairways identify the stupa type as one that commemorates the Tushita heavens, the perfected land in which the bodhisattva, Maitreya, dwells. Since devotees may aspire to be reborn within the Tushita heavens and Maitreya will one day descend from his idyllic land to herald a paradise on earth for all beings, the stairway conveys the mutual interpenetrability of a Buddhist heaven with our phenomenal world.

By omitting markers that would allow the viewer to perceive the size of the stupas eroding back into the earth from which they were built, Izu's composition creates a powerful aura of mystery (1999).

5.9 **Dunhuang Caves, China**

The subtle tonalities of this platinum print
make apparent the eroded softness of crumbling
stone and the drift of desert sands at the
Buddhist caves of Dunhuang, China. Izu's inti-
mate focus on a group of small caves set within
a cliff and his inclusion of the devotee's path at
the foreground of the composition emphasize
both the efforts of individuals to shape the phenomenal world in which they live and the
countless journeys taken to understand its more
profound realities (2000).

5.10 **Bezeklik Caves, Turfan, China**

Izu's panoramic vista depicting a lush riverine valley flanked by cliffs honeycombed with Buddhist caves makes visible the interconnectedness of secular and religious culture along the Silk Road. The gentry of the oasis settlements commissioned the construction of Buddhist caves and monasteries to accrue spiritual merit and social status. Here too, merchants exchanged goods, gathered provisions for the difficult treks across desert wastelands, and sought to secure their well-being by offering luxury items to the Buddhist community. The monasteries themselves were cosmopolitan complexes in which monks from East, Central, South, and West Asia gathered to transmit and study the Buddha's teachings (2000).

5.11 **Xi Xia Royal Tombs, Yinchuan, China**

Rising like mysterious sand castles from the
desert floor, the tombs (*wangling*) of Xi Xia
dynasty emperors and their most important
officials are all that remain of a spectacular
necropolis. The emperors had adopted the
Chinese practice of constructing tombs for the
commemoration and veneration of ancestors
when they conquered the region around present-day Yinchuan (Ningxia Province, China) in
the ninth century. At its peak, the Xi Xia
empire extended from the kingdom of Tibet
northward to Liao territory and southward to

Song China. Izu's crystalline detail and his subtly restricted palette of gray tones evoke the arid
desert and sand-filled windstorms that rounded
these once octagonal tombs (2000).

SACRED SITES ALONG THE SILK ROAD

Despite the Silk Road's venerable origins and legendary history, modern science is telling us much today that is new about the great route: its ancient formation, the people who traveled it, and its myriad cultural, commercial, and technological exchanges. Geology, archaeology, chemistry, metallurgy, and biology are among those fields that are offering insights into the Silk Road. The Silk Road itself has served as a conduit for transmission of scientific and technological understanding over the millennia and affords a modern analogy to globalization.

SIX • TRAVELING TECHNOLOGIES   MERTON C. FLEMINGS

MOVING CONTINENTS   Two hundred million years ago, the great supercontinent called Pangea had broken into several smaller continents. The era of the dinosaurs was beginning. One hundred twenty million years ago, one of those continents, which was to become what we know today as India, was located five thousand kilometers south of Asia, traveling northward at a speed of about ten centimeters per year. While India was on its way north, the great extinction of the dinosaurs and many other species took place. By forty million years ago,

Detail, Ritual wine server, China, Shang dynasty. See fig. 6.2

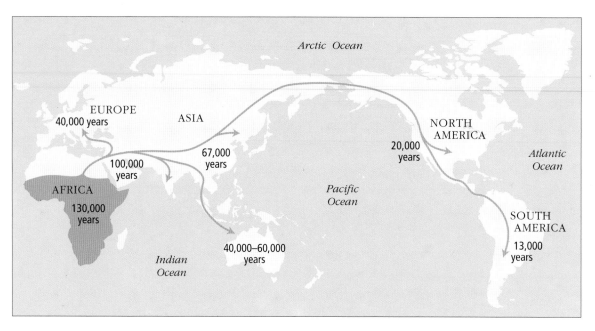

6.1 Map showing arrows and dates representing human migrations. (Adapted from *Nature* 408, December 7, 2000, p. 653).

India had collided with Asia.[1] At various times thereafter, glaciers covered much of Northern Europe and the mountainous regions of Silk Road lands. Especially during the colder and drier periods of these repeated glaciations, winds picked up and carried large quantities of dust across Asia. Accumulations of this fine dust, sometimes ninety meters thick, make up not only the deserts but also the fertile plains of central China. This dust also brings color to the Yellow River.

Early hominids were walking upright in Africa 2.5 million years ago. Some of these early hominids later constituted the first small wave of human movement across Asia; no doubt many traveled along what was to become the Silk Road. They evolved slowly over the succeeding millennia, DNA studies tell us. Anatomically modern humans, *Homo sapiens sapiens,* originated in Africa and began to spread outwards about one hundred thousand years ago. By seventy thousand years ago, these modern humans had spread across the Silk Road region, replacing completely the earlier hominids.[2] Figure 6.1 shows these migrations schematically.

Ten thousand years ago, as the existing glaciers receded to the north, farming began in West Asia. Some researchers, employing both results of DNA and linguistic studies, believe that farming later moved eastward at the rate of a kilometer or two a year, not by word of mouth but by migration of individuals who married local people and stayed to farm while their children moved eastward, migrating along what would later be called the Silk Road. However, farming appears to have been developed independently in several other areas of the globe, including Southeast Asia.

Geologic studies show that there was a great flood about seventy-five hundred years ago, near where agriculture began, in Mesopotamia. The flood was the result of a sudden pouring of water from the Mediterranean Sea into the Black Sea, through a narrow strait. This massive influx of water, a torrent apparently equivalent to two hundred Niagara Falls, extended the shores of the Black Sea at one to two kilometers per day. The geologists who first showed evidence of this flood proposed that perhaps it became a part of folk memory, inspiring the Babylonian flood myth in the epic of Gilgamesh, and later the biblical story of Noah. It is intriguing to imagine that this flood might even have helped propel our farming ancestors along the Silk Road.[3]

While most do not doubt the geological evidence of the deluge, archaeologists remain skeptical of any relation to Noah. What is exciting about this and other controversial theories of developments in Silk Road lands is that scientists today from diverse disciplines such as geology, linguistics, biology, and archaeology are meeting and working together in interdisciplinary teams to shed new light on old issues. Such teams are teaching us not only about geologically ancient eras but also about much more recent times, from the development of great cities and the flowering of the Bronze and Iron Ages to the development of machines and mechanical devices. These studies are providing a fresh understanding of the enormous historical importance of the routes we can call the Silk Road in the transmission of knowledge as well as culture and material goods.

DEVELOPMENT AND TRANSFER OF TECHNOLOGIES   Knowledge of glass manufacture began in the Mediterranean and spread to Asia during the middle of the first millennium B.C.E. Silk-making technology originated in China, probably by the second millennium B.C.E., although knowledge about the technique of sericulture did not reach the West (Byzantium) until 600 C.E. Copper smelting almost certainly began in West Asia by the fourth millennium B.C.E. and moved eastward, while in later years other metallurgical advances, notably in iron- and steelmaking, moved westward.

Printing originated in China, with movable type employed as early as 1045. Printing is thought to have diffused to the West as a result of the Mongol invasions that reached Europe by the late thirteenth century, since woodblock printing appeared in Germany a short time later. Printing with both a press and movable type began in Europe with Johannes Gutenberg in 1458. Gunpowder was known in China at least as early as the ninth century, but did not reach the West for another five hundred years.

Many other transmissions of technology can also be traced to the Silk Road, including the escapement, so essential for all mechanical clockwork. The Chinese were making mechanical clocks by the eleventh century C.E., three hundred years before the Europeans. The development of the eccentric connecting rod and piston rod, so essential for modern machines, goes back in China to the sixth century C.E. However, of all the technologies that moved between East and West, metallurgy is one of the most

6.2 Ritual wine server (*guang*), China, Shang dynasty, 12th century B.C.E. Bronze, height 17.8, width 19.2, depth 8.7 cm. Arthur M. Sackler Gallery, Smithsonian Institution, Washington, D.C., gift of Arthur M. Sackler, S87.0279a,b

studied for the reason that its archaeological record has withstood well the ravages of time. Advances in radiocarbon dating of organic materials associated with metallurgical finds often permit precise dating of those finds. Archaeometallurgy has much to tell us about the development and transfer of metallurgical technology across Silk Road lands.

ARCHAEOMETALLURGY "Modern" metallurgy was born in West Asia, with the development and employment by at least the mid-fourth millennium B.C.E. of the smelted copper alloys. "Arsenical copper" (copper mixed with a small percentage of arsenic) was apparently the first copper alloy. Found in excavations of the early city-states in the Tigris-Euphrates Delta, the earliest true bronzes (copper alloyed with a few percent tin) appeared in the early third millennium B.C.E. in ancient Mesopotamia. The royal graves

at Ur, for example, which date from the Early Dynastic period, or to about 2600 B.C.E., contained bronzes of 8 to 10 percent tin.[4] As tin bronze became the preferred alloy (because of its ability both to lower the melting point and to increase the strength of the metal), the production of such castings depended on trade along one part of what was to become the Silk Road: the required copper ore came from deposits across the Anatolian and Iranian highlands, and the location

6.3 Ritual wine container (*bohuan you*), China, Western Zhou dynasty, 11th–10th centuries B.C.E. Bronze, height 38.1, width 30.1, depth 23 cm. Arthur M. Sackler Gallery, Smithsonian Institution, Washington, D.C., gift of Arthur M. Sackler, S87.0333a, b

of the tin ores was even more restricted. There can be no doubt as to the importance of bronze with respect to the development of societies of the time. Certainly its impact on warfare is well documented in biblical times:

> And there came out from the camp of the Philistines a champion named Goliath, of
> Gath, whose height was six cubits and a span. He had a helmet of bronze on his head,

and he was armed with a coat of mail, and the weight of the coat was five thousand shekels of bronze. And he had greaves of bronze upon his legs, and a javelin of bronze slung between his shoulders.[5]

6.4 Graduated set of six ritual bells (zhong), China, Eastern Zhou dynasty, 6th century B.C.E. Bronze, heights range from 25.5 to 43 cm. Arthur M. Sackler Gallery, Smithsonian Institution, Washington, D.C., gift of Arthur M. Sackler, S87.0004–9.

Copper alloys appeared in Central Asia in the third and early second millennia B.C.E., well after their development in West Asia. Over the past decades, scholars have debated intensely whether individual technologies "diffused" from one region to another in these ancient times, or were independently discovered. Nowhere has this discussion been more vigorous than in the case of whether copper metallurgy diffused eastward into Central Asia and China or was invented independently in one or more locations there. Scholars continue to debate the issue, but evidence is accumulating for strong east-west connections in the development of metallurgy across Silk Road lands. Of course, that is made all the more believable by the growing evidence of human movement along the Silk Road from earliest times, as discussed by Elizabeth Barber in Chapter 3.

For many years it was thought that the earliest East Asian bronze industry of significance occurred in the Shang dynasty[6] (ca. 1600–1050 B.C.E.). The Shang culture had a long and magnificent bronze-casting tradition that produced some of the largest and most sophisticated bronze objects of the entire ancient world. Figure 6.2 is a late Shang wine vessel, and figure 6.3 a slightly later Zhou dynasty (1050–221 B.C.E.) bronze wine container. Both show elaborate design and sophisticated workmanship. Figure 6.4 shows a graduated set of six ritual bells similar to ones on the famous chime of sixty-five bells (ca. 433 B.C.E.) recovered from the tomb of Marquis Yi of Zeng. Replications of the Marquis Yi chime bells were used in Tan Dun's Symphony 1997 written for the changeover ceremonies in Hong Kong and Beijing, marking the end of British rule in Hong Kong.

We now understand that a flourishing bronze- and copper-casting industry existed in China prior to the Shang dynasty, and a number of clues suggest a strong link of this earlier industry to technology from West Asia. These clues include the newer findings of connections among cultures of the Eurasian steppes, connections that would very likely have carried known copper and bronze technology from adjacent regions into northwest China. On the technical side, additional evidence is provided by the discovery of arsenic-containing copper and bronze pieces from northwest China dated as early as 1800 B.C.E. Arsenical alloys are the earliest copper alloys found to the west, but are not found eastward at all, and so these alloys strongly suggest a technological link to West Asia.[7] We may today conclude with some confidence that the prehistoric Silk Road was key to the spread of copper and bronze technology from West to Central Asia to northwest China and the North China Plain. Of course, Chinese artisans made many improvements in the technology, including development of the "piece-mold" casting process, carrying the foundry art to an extraordinary height.

IRON AND STEEL TECHNOLOGIES   Meteoritic iron was in use sporadically in the eastern Mediterranean from as early as 5000 B.C.E., but only after about 1200 B.C.E. did the smelting of iron ore become widely practiced and iron widely used. A letter from Hatusilis III, king of the Hittites, to Shalmaneser I of Assyria in the mid-thirteenth century B.C.E., reads:

> As for the good iron you wrote me about, good iron in Kuzzuwatna in my seal house is not available. It is a bad time for producing iron, as I have written. They will produce good iron, but so far they have not finished. When they have finished I will send it to you. Today I am having an iron dagger brought to you.[8]

By the tenth century B.C.E., iron was in common use in most of West Asia for utilitarian and military applications. Iron is produced from mined iron ore by reacting the ore with a form of carbon, usually charcoal. Throughout antiquity and down to the fourteenth century C.E., the iron employed in West Asia and Europe was produced in furnaces known as smelting furnaces that never reached temperatures above about eight hundred fifty degrees Celsius. Pure iron, however, melts at about fifteen hundred degrees Celsius. Thus, the iron that resulted from this smelting operation was never liquefied. The iron ore was chemically changed to a pasty solid iron mass that had to be wrought, or worked, while still hot, to achieve a useful engineering material. The pasty mass is referred to as "bloom," and the ancient factories producing it are known as "bloomeries."

What we term "steel" is iron with small quantities of other elements added (most notably carbon in amounts of about 0.1 to 0.8 percent). Much of the early steelmaker's art revolved around controlling the exact amount of carbon in the iron and also controlling how the metal was heated, cooled, and "worked," since these factors all strongly influence the strength and serviceability of steel. Steel, almost uniquely among metals, becomes extremely hard when it is properly heated and then rapidly cooled in water or oil. That the early steelmakers understood this sequence is evidenced not only by metallurgical finds but by writings such as Book IX of the *Odyssey* describing how Odysseus and his men blinded Polyphemus the cyclops with a hot stake:

> Seizing the olive stake, sharp at the tip, they plunged it in his eye, and I, perched above, whirled it around. . . . The vapor singed off all his lids on the two sides, and

even his brows, as the ball burned and its roots crackled in the flame. As when a smith dips a great axe or adze into cold water, hissing to temper it—for that is strength to iron—so hissed his eye about the olive stake.[9]

The development of iron metallurgy in Asia has been a matter of debate among scholars for some time. It now seems most likely, however, that the technology of iron smelting diffused from West Asia through Siberia into China by about the eighth century B.C.E., possibly transmitted by Scythian nomads. What is remarkable is how quickly the technology flowered in China over the succeeding few centuries. Then, by the fourth century B.C.E., Chinese artisans had made a remarkable advance in the technology. They developed and began to employ "blast" furnaces capable of reaching temperatures much higher than those achieved in Western furnaces. Blast furnaces employ bellows to force air into a bed of the raw materials employed in iron production: a heated carbonaceous substance and iron ore. The forced air increases the burning rate of the carbon, and with enough air, raises the temperature to above eleven hundred degrees Celsius. A seventeenth-century Chinese industrial text illustrates the basic furnace type first used much earlier (fig. 6.5). The bellows were originally hand powered, as illustrated in this figure, and were later water powered.

6.5 Chinese blast furnace, 17th century (from the 17th-century industrial text, *Tiangong kaiwu* [Exploitation of the works of nature] by Song Yingxing). Translated by E-tu Zen Sun and Shiou-chuan Sun. (University Park, Pa., Pennsylvania State University, 1966). Copyright 1966 by the Pennsylvania State University. Reproduced by permission of the publisher.

6.6 Han dynasty cast iron stove (from B. L. Simpson, *Development of the Metal Casting Industry* [Chicago: American Foundrymen's Society, 1948], p. 31). Permission to reprint granted by the American Foundry Society, Des Plaines, Illinois

6.7 This large cast iron lion, cast in China about 953 C.E., still stands in a monastery yard near Cangzhou, Hebei Province. The lion measures 5 meters in length and 6 meters in height; it was cast in small sections. Metal thickness, 50 to 200 mm (from B. L. Simpson, *Development of the Metal Casting Industry* [Chicago: American Foundrymen's Society, 1948], p. 38). Permission to reprint granted by the American Foundry Society, Des Plaines, Illinois

This temperature of eleven hundred degrees Celsius is not high enough to melt pure iron or steel, but when iron contains 3–4 percent carbon and perhaps a little silicon, its melting point is reduced to that attainable by these blast furnaces. Thus cast iron was born, a new substance capable of being made fully molten and of being poured into molds to produce objects. Cast iron soon became a material of choice for many craftspeople. Agricultural implements, thin-wall cooking pots, and other industrial goods were produced in many small foundries throughout East Asia centuries before cast iron arrived in Europe. Figure 6.6, for example, shows a cast iron stove of the Han dynasty (206 B.C.E.–220 C.E.), with an inscription that reads: "May it please your Lords." By 1100, cast iron was so prevalent that it was used to roof pagodas and other structures, and this was still three hundred years before it appeared in the West. The magnificent six-meter-high cast iron lion of figure 6.7, cast in Hebei Province about 953 C.E., exemplifies the technology of the time.

6.8 Scene from an early Western iron foundry, depicting metal melted in a blast furnace and being poured into a sand mold for stove-plate work. A water powered bellows (not shown) is behind the furnace (from B. L. Simpson, *Development of the Metal Casting Industry* [Chicago: American Foundrymen's Society, 1948], p. 153). Permission to reprint granted by the American Foundry Society, Des Plaines, Illinois

Chinese artisans, faced with the new material, cast iron, proceeded to develop innovative ways to modify it. They learned to alter its internal structure to improve its strength and ductility by a complex metallurgical process we call malleabilization, a process we use in the West today. More important, as a result of the ability to produce this liquid cast iron, steelmaking technology in China took a much different path from that in the West. By at least the second century B.C.E., Chinese were able to produce steel by starting with liquid cast iron and reducing its carbon content.

Throughout this long period from the fourth century B.C.E. to well into the second millennium C.E., the cast iron blast furnace was unknown in Europe. Steel continued to be produced from ore by the "blooming" process described earlier. The cast iron blast furnace arrived in Europe only sometime after the thirteenth century (fig. 6.8). Manuscript evidence points to 1380 C.E. for its arrival in the Rhine Valley. Several processes, long known in China for producing wrought iron and steel, then surfaced over the next one to two hundred years. No direct evidence has yet emerged of transmission of the Chinese technology to Europe, but the eminent historian of Chinese science and technology, Joseph Needham, has pointed out that the appearance of all these correlated techniques within such a short period seems significant and suggests a diffusion of at least a stimulus from East Asia in the invention of the blast furnace. The Rhine Valley was also where the inventions of gunpowder and printing were implemented at about the same time. Thus, he notes, the mastery of cast iron takes its place among a number of other European adoptions of East Asian techniques in what has been called the "Fourteenth-Century Cluster."[10]

For as much as two thousand years, up to perhaps the eighteenth century, China's iron industry was the world's largest and most technically advanced. But by 1900, with the advent of large-scale, efficient processes in the West, the Chinese could no longer compete with foreign ironworks. The industry then entered a period of decline that has lasted to almost the present time. Today, iron technology in China is being revitalized by technology flowing along the metaphoric Silk Road from Japan, Korea, and the United States. In spite of many political problems still existing across Silk Road lands, it is gratifying to see, after the long hiatus from the eighteenth century, growing scientific, technological, and cultural interchanges across these regions.

THE SILK ROAD TODAY   As Yo-Yo Ma states in the first chapter of this volume, there is no better modern metaphor for the Silk Road than the Internet. A nationwide system of local Internet service providers was completed in China in 1998, and now the seven westernmost provinces have joined the more populated parts of China on the World Wide Web. News articles chronicle the spread of the Internet across the Silk Road. The *New York Times,* in March 2000, describes a one-room Internet bar in Kashgar, Bright Sheng's destination on his musical travels, discussed in Chapter 2. In this bar, eight personal computers are strung together with a tangle of wires, a coal burning stove in the room spewing black smoke but failing to raise the temperature to a comfortable level. In the monastery town of Xiahe in Gansu Province, Internet users in similar surroundings look out a window at mule-drawn carts and nomadic herdsman who trudge along the town's one main street. It is exciting to see these Internet users in Kashgar and Xiahe, on the traditional Silk Road, becoming part of the new, metaphorical Silk Road.[11]

Both the lack of infrastructure and the concerns of China's leadership will limit the growth rate of the Internet, but its continued spread is surely unstoppable. An article in the *New York Times* speaks specifically of three new "Roads" across Asia; B2B (Business-to-Business), B2C (Business-to-Consumer), and C2C (Consumer-to-Consumer):

> Somewhere in the Turkish highlands this summer, a camper will bed for the night with a Chinese-made tent and sleeping bag, courtesy of a Turkish sporting goods wholesaler who bought hundreds over the Internet from a Chinese company earlier this year. It is the kind of transaction that many people hope is the beginning of a revolution for China's formidable economy.[12]

We need not, today, limit our metaphorical Silk Road by geography. Interpreting today's metaphoric Silk Road in the broadest sense, we can say that technological exchanges continue in the multiple interactions represented by the industrial and technological globalization of our time, in transportation, materials, information technologies, and the life sciences. The flow of information is for all practical purposes instantaneous in the news, financial, and technological arenas. In science and technology, a discovery announced in one part of the world will find, often within days, researchers throughout the globe testing the results or conducting new experiments based on the results. It is widely recognized today that the newer distant communication technologies have much promise for collaborative research and education as well, and this author has been deeply involved in such a metaphoric Silk Road venture for the past four years—the Singapore-MIT Alliance.

VIRTUAL REALITY   Technological developments of just the last few years make it possible now for a lecturer in Cambridge, Massachusetts, to speak directly to a group of students halfway around the world, to be visible to them on a screen in full size, to "see" each student and respond to his or her question (fig. 6.9). The student soon adapts to the virtual reality and adopts a behavior not greatly different from classroom behavior if the lecturer were in the same room. Using this technology, the Massachusetts Institute of Technology, along with two Singaporean institutions—the National University of Singapore and the Nanyang Technological University—have developed the largest global educational partnership in the world today, the Singapore-MIT Alliance (SMA). This multiyear effort aims to foster collaborations in graduate education and research. Students enrolled in the program can receive a professional master's degree, a thesis master's degree, or a Ph.D. in one of five modern engineering fields.

Most lectures are beamed live, through a noncommercial Internet channel, in a synchronous, two-way communication mode using state-of-the-art lecture facilities

6.9 MIT professor lecturing to students in Singapore

available both at MIT and in Singapore. These modern facilities enable the SMA student, sitting in a lecture room exactly halfway around the globe, to participate in live classroom discussions, along with MIT students. The transmission vehicle is Internet II, a noncommercial broadband medium. In addition to lecture material disseminated ahead to the student electronically, spontaneous electronic communication during the lecture is facilitated by electronic writing tablets with color imaging features, electronic white boards, and software with high-speed animation capabilities. Students in their dormitory rooms can access lecture notes, assignments, homework, reading material, textbooks, digital videotapes of prior lectures and laboratory demonstrations, as well as example problems and solutions to homework through the course Website. Interactions with the teaching assistants and professors, individually as well as in groups, are facilitated through Web chat rooms and video-conferencing. Similar one-on-one or group interactions over the Internet are key to the research interactions among students and professors that form an important part of graduate engineering education.

Close and instantaneous interactions such as the Singapore-MIT Alliance, made possible by modern information technologies, will enhance the flow of ideas all over the globe in the decades ahead in a profound way. We may hope the impact of this will be as great on advancing the development of civilization as was the historic Silk Road. •

The author wishes to thank Robert Murowchick for providing important contributions to the content of this chapter, particularly relating to early bronze metallurgy. Thanks also to Martha Goodway for her helpful comments.

1   Peter Cattermole, *Building Planet Earth,* (Cambridge: Cambridge University Press, 2000), p. 40.

2   S. Blair Hedges, "A Start for Population Genomics," *Nature* 408 (2000): 652–53.

3   Richard A. Kerr, "Black Sea Deluge May Have Helped Farming," *Science* 279 (1998): 1132. See also John Noble Wilford, "Experts Face Off on Noah's Flood," *New York Times,* January 9, 2001, p. D6.

4   Stephen L. Sass, *The Substance of Civilization* (New York: Arcade Publishing, 1998), p. 49.

5   I Samuel 17:4–7, cited in ibid., p. 90.

6   Max Loehr, "Weapons and Tools from Anyang, and Siberian Analogies," *American Journal of Archaeology* 53 (1949): 129. See also Max Loehr, *Chinese Bronze Age Weapons* (Ann Arbor: University of Michigan Press, 1956), pp. 103–5.

7   Sun Shuyun and Han Rubin, "A Study of Casting and Manufacturing Techniques of Early Copper and Bronze Artifacts Found in Gansu," *Wenwu,* 1997, no. 7:75–84. Thorough discussions in English of the recent work on Xinjiang's Bronze Age include Jianjun Mei, *Copper and Bronze Metallurgy in Late Prehistoric Xinjiang.* BAR International Series 865 (Oxford: Archaeopress, 2000); and the various articles included in Fredrik Hiebert and Nicola Di Cosmo, eds., "Between Lapis and Jade: Ancient Cultures of Central Asia," *Anthropology & Archaeology of Eurasia* 34, no. 4 (Spring 1996).

8   Quoted in Sass, *Substance of Civilization,* p. 90.

9   Homer, trans. George Herbert Palmer, *The Odyssey of Homer,* book 2 (Boston: Houghton Mifflin, 1886), p. 305.

10 Joseph Needham, "The Evolution of Iron and Steel Technology in East and Southeast Asia," in *The Coming of the Age of Iron,* ed. Theodore A. Wertime and James D. Muhly (New Haven and London: Yale University Press, 1980), pp. 507–39. See also Katheryn M. Linduff, "Metallurgists in Ancient East Asia: The Chinese and Who Else?" in *The Beginnings of Metallurgy in China,* ed, Katheryn M. Linduff, Han Rubin, and Sun Shuyun (Lewiston, Queenston: Edwin Mellen Press, 2000), pp. 1–28.

11 Jennifer Lee, "Tracking the Web Across China," *New York Times,* March 29, 2000.

12 Craig S. Smith, "Online Overseas: Three Roads in China: B2B, B2C, and C2C," *New York Times,* June 7, 2000.

Iranian cinema has one of the longest histories in the

regions traversed by the Silk Road, and it has benefited

and suffered from the cultural exchanges its position

at the crossroads of trade, over rich deposits of oil,

has generated.

THE RISE OF THE CINEMA The first footage by an Iranian

was filmed in 1900, the first public cinema was opened

by Catholic missionaries in Tabriz in the same year,

and the first commercial cinema began operation in

1904 in Tehran. Until 1930, this cinema was dominated

entirely by the production of silent, nonfiction films. In

1932 Ovanes Ohanian, an Armenian-Iranian, directed *Mr.*

Hajji, The Movie Actor (*Hajji Aqa, Aktur-i Cinema*, 1932),

Iran's first full-length feature fiction film. Technically

sophisticated but silent, the film tells the story of a tradi-

tional religious man (hajji) who is transformed from hat-

ing cinema to proclaiming its value in improving the lot of

Iranians. Self-consciously but delightfully, *Mr. Hajji* deals

head-on with the moral panic of the clerics and the tradi-

Bashu, The Little Stranger,
1985. See fig. 7.2.a.

tionalists who feared the corrupting influences of cinema.

123

Ethnic and religious minorities, particularly Armenians, were instrumental in developing the nascent Iranian cinema, and a number of film pioneers, like Ohanian, were hyphenated Iranians or émigrés from Russia and the Caucasus regions in the path of the Silk Road. Many had been educated abroad and were connected to the ruling elite or the merchant class. Significantly, Iranian cinema benefited not only from the interethnicity, immigration, and Western education of its filmmakers but also from exchanges with neighboring Silk Road countries.

These exchanges became more prominent in the sound era. For example, a Turkish photographer in Turkey filmed the first Persian-language sound newsreel, shown widely in Iran in 1932. In it the Iranian prime minister Mohammed Ali Forughi confers with Kemal Ataturk and delivers a brief speech in Persian, astonishing audiences unaccustomed to hearing Persian spoken on the screen. The first Persian-language sound feature, *The Lur Girl* (*Dukhtar-i Lur,* 1933), written by Iranian expatriate poet Abdul-Husayn Sepenta, was directed in India by Ardeshir Irani. The film, a melodramatic love story that extolled Iranian nationalism and modernization under Riza Shah Pahlavi (reigned 1925–41), was highly successful with Iranians. From his base in India, Sepenta went on to direct for export a succession of talkies based on Iranian epics, such as *Firdawsi* (1934), on the life of the famous poet who composed the massive *Shahnama* (Book of kings), and classic love stories such as *Shirin u Farhad* (1936) and *Layli u Majnun* (1937). These epics and love stories were widely known among the Persian-speaking peoples living in the countries along the Silk Road. But in form and theme, these films resembled the Indian popular genre of "epicals."

In 1948 Esmail Kushan directed *The Tempest of Life (Tufan-e Zindigi),* the first Persian-language feature made inside Iran. The success of his films, produced at his Pars Film Studio, prompted a rejuvenation of the local industry and a proliferation of new studios. This rejuvenation was also encouraged by the stifling censorship of the early 1940s, which blocked the distribution of many foreign films, especially those showing revolutions, riots, and strikes as well as indecency, pacifism, or anti-Islamic attitudes.[1]

The global ascendancy of the United States after World War II had a profound impact on documentary film in Iran. As part of U.S. policy to win the hearts and minds of people in noncommunist countries, especially those, like Iran, bordering the Soviet Union, the United States Information Agency began an ambitious project of film production. Under its auspices, American professors and filmmakers, known as the Syracuse University team, visited Iran in the early 1950s to establish 16mm film-processing laboratories and train filmmakers, who then made scores of documentary and educational films. The team also developed a pro-shah, pro-American newsreel called *Iran News (Akhbar-i Iran),* 402 issues of which were shown in public theaters throughout the country.[2]

THE MODERN PAHLAVI ERA   The 1960s were tumultuous years for Iran, bringing both the freedom that petro-dollars and globalization of capital promised and the restrictions that they also entailed. The political consolidation of Muhammad Riza Shah's regime (1941–79) involved the centralization and expansion of the state security apparatus and state control over the film industry. Socially conscious films made by young, European-educated filmmakers met with official disapproval and confiscation. Farrokh Gaffary's *South of the City* (*Jonub-i Shahr,* 1958), for example, which realistically depicts life in the poverty-stricken southern district of Tehran, was, according to the director, not only banned but also had its negative mutilated.[3]

The ambition of the shah and the ruling elite to modernize Iran rapidly along a Western trajectory meshed with the interests of American film and television industries in expanding their markets worldwide. Global media interests thus replaced regional influences in Iran. American companies, such as MGM, RCA, and NBC-TV, began selling all kinds of products and services, from feature films to television programs, from television receivers to television studios, from communication expertise to personnel training: in short, they sold not only consumer products but also consumer ideology.

At the reception end, however, regional influences remained strong. Egyptian and Indian melodramas and song-and-dance films were very popular with moviegoers, and the thriving market for their songs intensified the hold of these films on the popular imagination. Record companies and radio stations, which promoted these songs, became part of a developing popular culture industry whose contents were highly influenced by regional and Western products.

At the end of the 1960s, the local film industry, which had been producing scores of low-quality melodramas, comedies, and tough-guy (*luti*) films was jolted by the release of two films that set a new trend, later called the New Wave. Masud Kimiai's *Qaysar* (1969) polished the *luti* genre by developing a strong binary opposition of good guy versus bad guy and by linking the good with Iranian tradition and culture and the bad with its violations (which in some circles was interpreted as Westernization and secularization). Thus the tough-guy genre's revenge plot, usually involving defense of a kinswoman, was coded to be read as involving defense of Iranian authenticity. Kimiai also intensified the pacing of the genre by using an action-oriented filming style, dramatic camera angles, and stirring music.

The other film that shook the local film industry and audiences was Dariush Mehrjui's *Cow* (*Gav,* 1969). It tells the story of a farmer who, upon losing his cow, the sole source of his livelihood, begins to embody it spiritually and physically; he goes mad and eventually dies a dramatic death (see fig. 7.1). The story was by a leading dissident writer, Ghulam-Husayn Saedi, and the film heralded a new alliance between socially

7.1 *The Cow,* 1969   conscious filmmakers and writers. In doing so, it also revived the social realist trend that Gaffary had begun more than a decade before. *The Cow*'s focus on villagers was seen as a return to roots, echoing in a different genre the tough-guy films' return to the authentic bedrock of Iranian society and psychology. Its honest treatment of Iranian life and sparse style were considered a breath of fresh air.

The Cow embodied the contradictions that became the hallmark of New Wave films: its sponsorship by the state and its censorship by the state. The Ministry of Culture and Art withheld the film's release, fearing it would contradict "the official image of Iran as a modern nation of promise and plenty."[4] However, when the film was unofficially entered in the Venice International Film Festival in 1969 and garnered a top award, the ministry lifted the ban. From then on, international festivals became players in the Iranian politics of cinema. Indeed, the international and subsequent national success of *The Cow* opened the way for government support of art cinema. Cinema was seen as a means for Iran to gain a positive international profile at a time when Iranian students abroad were highly critical of their government. This uneasy alliance produced a succession of important films, such as Bahram Baizai's *Downpour* (*Ragbar,* 1970) and Mehrjui's *Postman* (*Pustchi,* 1970).

New Wave films gave impetus to, and were part of, a complex film culture that evolved between the late 1960s and the revolution of 1978–79. Trusted royal relatives headed both the Ministry of Culture and Art and the National Iranian Radio and Television, which benefited from increasing national oil revenues. Both supported documentaries and fictional cinema and heavily invested in cultural festivals. Film clubs screened and discussed canonical films. Festivals showcased and gave awards to local talent and exposed Iranians to outstanding examples of foreign films, and the cultural arms of many foreign embassies also regularly exhibited important films from their countries. The government entered filmmaking through investment by state-run enterprises, such as the Institute for Intellectual Development of Children and Young Adults, Telfilm, and Film Industry Development Company, which together produced some of the best films of the period.

The Iranian film culture was given a boost by a group of foreign-trained filmmakers, such as Hajir Dariush, Bahman Farmanara, and Sohrab Shahid-Saless, some of whom collaborated with respected antigovernment writers, such as Sadiq Chubak, Mahmud Dawlatabadi, Hushang Golshiri, and Saedi. The films they produced moved away from traditional genres in favor of increased realism, individual character psychology, and higher technical quality. Film schools and a Super-8 film network called Free Cinema (*Cinema-yi Azad*) trained many new filmmakers. Finally, an independent collective of New Wave filmmakers, unhappy with state intervention in cinema, formed the New Film Group, which produced Mehrjui's scathing *Cycle* (*Dayira-yi Mina*, 1974) and Saless's poetically austere *Still Life* (*Tabiat-i Bijan*, 1975).

Despite this apparently healthy film culture, by the mid-1970s the socioeconomic basis of the film industry had begun to crumble. Import laws had made it more lucrative to import films than to produce them locally, and nearly a quarter of box-office receipts were lost to taxes. Inflation pushed up the cost of raw stock, equipment, services, and salaries, while imperial decree kept the ticket prices for this most popular entertainment form deliberately low. Interest rates were so high that even a short delay between a film's completion and its screening could drive the producer into bankruptcy, and the widespread censorship of political themes meant that completed films often had to wait months, even years, for an exhibition permit. This situation not only jeopardized the financial status of producers but also made the directors timid about the issues they chose to tackle.

Ironically, New Wave films had an indirectly adverse effect on local film production by fragmenting the audience. Tired of formula song-and-dance or tough-guy films, some filmgoers sought out the work of New Wave filmmakers who, due to strict censorship, were unable to meet expectations. Unsatisfied by the heavily compromised films or by the abstruse filmic language necessary to evade censorship, this audience turned back to foreign films. Also, direct government involvement in filmmaking added an extra level of competition and undermined the healthy growth of the independent, commercially driven industry.

THE CONSOLIDATION OF CINEMA   In the early days of revolution, cinema was condemned for what was widely perceived to be its support of the Pahlavi regime's Westernization projects. Traditionalists charged that cinema was an agent of cultural colonization by the West, and it became a favorite target of revolutionary wrath. In August 1978, nearly four hundred spectators perished in a fire deliberately set by anti-shah forces in the Rex theater in Abadan. Soon burning cinemas were integral to the dismantling of the shah's regime. By the time the Islamic government was installed in 1979, 180 cinemas had been destroyed, creating a shortage of exhibition sites from which Iranian cinema still suffers.[5]

In this purification process imports were curtailed, and those foreign films already in the country were reviewed, with the overwhelming majority judged as failing to meet the evolving Islamic values. Of the 898 foreign films produced in this period, 531—most of them from the West—were rejected. Of 2,208 locally produced films reviewed, 1,956 were denied exhibition permits.[6] Many films were made appropriate through strategic editing of scenes containing nudity or what was defined as immodesty. When cutting confused the narrative, offensive body parts were blocked off with markers applied to each frame. Entertainers, actors, and filmmakers were also subjected to purification, involving harassment, legal charges, incarceration, expropriation of possessions, and the barring of their faces, voices, and bodies from the screen. Uncertainty about what was allowed led to a general absence of women from films.

7.2a Bashu, The Little Stranger, 1985   Few films of quality were made in the early days, but there were

exceptions, including Amir Naderi's *Search* (*Justuju,* 1980) and two films from Baizai:
Tara's Ballad (*Chirika-yi Tara,* 1980) and *Yazdigird's Death* (*Marg-i Yazdigird,* 1982).
The latter two were banned then and are banned now.

During the revolutionary upheavals, some filmmakers fled the country. Soon a
large contingent of film people, entertainers, performers, and artists had turned Los
Angeles into a center of Iranian popular culture.[7] Over the years, Iranians made more
films outside their country of origin than any other displaced group from a nation
through which the Silk Road passed. Even though these filmmakers worked in different
countries, their output was so large and diverse in form and style—documentaries,
fiction films, music videos, animated films, avant-garde videos, and television shows—
that it constituted an Iranian cinema of exile and diaspora. Exploring the trauma and
tragedy of loss and displacement and the problem of identity formation, it is at once
Iranian "national cinema" and "accented cinema," the global cinema of exile and diaspora created by displaced filmmakers since the 1960s.[8]

It is important to note that the clerical leaders were not opposed to cinema per se:
they were against what religious leader Ayatollah Ruhollah Khomeini called its "misuse"
by the Pahlavi regime to "corrupt" and "subjugate" Iranians. To ensure that film was
used "properly," in June 1982 the cabinet approved a series of landmark regulations governing the exhibition of movies and videos and charged the Ministry of Culture and
Islamic Guidance (MCIG) with its enforcement.[9]

As before the revolution, political consolidation entailed   7.2b *Bashu, The Little Stranger,* 1985

7.3a *The Runner,* 1985   consolidation of culture. In 1983, the ministry created the Farabi Cinema Foundation to streamline and control the import and export of films and film equipment and supplies and to encourage local production. Many regulations codifying "Islamic values" as well as encouraging the production of quality films were put into effect. The municipal tax for local films was reduced, ticket prices were increased, and prices for importing equipment, film stock, and chemicals were calculated at the government-controlled exchange rate instead of at the floating rate, which was up to twenty times higher. In addition, producers and exhibitors gained a voice in assigning their films to theaters. All these measures centralized the regulative and enforcement authorities within the ministry. But they also rationalized cinema, and the number of films produced annually shot up almost threefold: from twenty-two features in 1983 to fifty-seven in 1986.

The new cinema that gradually emerged by the mid-1980s was both old and new. It was old in the sense that it benefited from the continuity provided by veterans of the Pahlavi-era cinema. Several key filmmakers were reinstated, and their high-quality films invigorated the postrevolutionary cinema. Among these were Baizai's *Bashu, The Little Stranger* (*Bashu, ghariba-yi kuchak,* 1985; figs 7.2a, b), Naderi's *Runner* (*Davanda,* 1985; figs. 7.3a, b), and Abbas Kiarostami's *Where Is the Friend's House?* (*Khana-yi dust kujast?,* 1986), which variously examined and critiqued the widespread displacement of Iranian populations, from the Persian Gulf to the Caspian Sea, by war, injustice, and foreign domination. Mehrjui's comedy *Tenants* (*Ijarihnishinha,* 1986) poked devastating fun at

housing problems in Tehran. This emerging art cinema was also new in the sense that a group of first-time directors, raised after the revolution, brought fresh ideas and concerns. Among them, Mohsen Makhmalbaf was the most controversial and versatile with such works as *The Peddler* (*Dastfurush*, 1986), a tripartite film that creates a hallucinatory world in the throes of chaos and disintegration.

The commercial success of high-quality art cinema films led banks to offer long-term loans for film production, putting parts of the industry on a more secure financial footing. The MCIG established a film-grading system favoring higher-quality films that could be exhibited in higher-class theaters in prime season and for longer periods, thus enhancing box-office receipts. The government also encouraged synch-sound filming by selling filmmakers who chose this method a third more raw stock at the cheaper government-controlled rate.

Production output fluctuated but remained high, with an average of more than fifty feature films a year in the 1990s. Art cinema films were aggressively entered in international film festivals, garnering high praise and many prizes, including Baizai's *Travelers* (*Musafiran*, 1992); Makhmalbaf's *Once Upon a Time, Cinema* (*Nasir al-Din Shah, aktur-i cinema*, 1992—fig. 7.4) and *Gabbeh* (1996); Mehrjui's *Hamoon* (1990—fig. 7.5) and *Layli* (1996); Kiarostami's *Close-Up* (*Kelosap: Namay-i Nazdik*, 1990); *Under the Olive Trees* (*Zir-e Darakhtan-i Zaytun*, 1994); and *The Wind Will Carry Us* (*Bad Ma Ra Khahad Burd*, 1999); Jafar Panahi's *White Balloon* (*Badkonak-i Sipid*, 1995); and Majid Majidi's *Color of Paradise* (*Rang-i Khuda*, 1999).

7.4 *Once Upon a Time, Cinema*, 1992   The increasing presence of women both before and behind the cameras added new dimensions to the emerging art cinema. Yet their representation was fraught with complex theological, ideological, political, and aesthetic considerations. In the 1980s a new grammar for filming women developed, involving shot composition, acting, touching, and relay of the gaze between male and female actors. In essence, the grammar encouraged a "modesty" of looking and acting and instituted an "averted look" instead of a direct gaze, particularly one imbued with sexual desire.[10] In the 1990s, women moved from the background of the stories and the shots into the foreground, and they were no longer confined to the home interiors but propelled into the streets and the workplace. The restrictive filming grammar was also liberalized. The averted gaze became more focused and direct, sometimes charged with sexual desire. Significantly, more women directors of feature films emerged in one decade after the revolution than in all the previous decades combined. Their best works included Rakhshan Banietemad's *Narges* (1992) and *May Lady* (*Banu-yi Urdibihisht*, 1998), Tahmineh Milani's *Two Women* and Samira Makhmalbaf's *Blackboard* (*Takhta Sia*, 2000).

As in the Pahlavi era, censorship remained a big problem for filmmakers. To receive an exhibition permit, all films had to undergo a four-phase approval process, of synopsis-screenplay, cast and crew, and completed film. While scrutiny at early phases has been eased, getting approval of the completed film remains a formidable obstacle.

By the late 1990s, many of the financial, regulative, technical, and production infrastructures necessary for sustaining a high level of film output were in place. However, the very success of these infrastructures, the doubling of the Iranian population in twenty years to more than 60 million, the relative cheapness of movie tickets compared to other entertainment forms, and the general popularity and prestige of cinema brought out the structural deficiencies in other sectors of the industry. Many theaters destroyed by revolutionary wrath were not rebuilt. Even if they had been, they could not accommodate the swelling population. At the start of 1993 there were 268 cinemas nationwide, one for every 209,000 people.[11] Projection and sound equipment had also deteriorated badly. The neglect of this sector of the industry was so profound that even conservative clerical leaders, such as the speaker of the Majles (parliament), urged action by declaring that the "religious reward" of building a cinema is equal to that of building a mosque.[12] However, the need for allocating massive sums to build and refurbish theaters came just when the national economy was in a tailspin, forcing the country to borrow, for the first time since the revolution, from foreign governments and the World Bank. In the aftermath of the Iran-Iraq War (1980–88) and the Persian Gulf War (1990–91), the government of Hashemi Rafsanjani attempted to rebuild the economy despite the American-led boycott of Iran. These attempts created panic in the film industry, particularly when the government's partial subsidy was eliminated.

In 1997, the former minister of culture and Islamic guidance, Mohammad Khatami, who had lost his position during the "cultural invasion" debate of the early

7.5 *Hamoon*, 1990

133

1990s, was elected president in a surprising landslide. Promising political reform, rule of law, tolerance, and cultural exchange with the West, he was supported overwhelmingly by women and young people. Filmmakers hoped that culture and cinema would receive special attention and the limits on public expression would be lifted—a hope dampened considerably by a judiciary decision in the late 1990s to ban dozens of reformist papers and jail their editors.

To restructure the shattered economy, in 1999 Khatami offered a five-year privatization plan that would reduce government involvement in, among other things, film financing, production, and exhibition. To deal with unauthorized uses of videos and satellite television, the government relinquished its monopoly on video distribution by licensing local film producers to import foreign films on video. Formerly the government had protected the local film industry from competition by essentially banning imports. To prevent unfair competition, the importing of foreign films was tied to the production of new local films. Accordingly, local producers could import four foreign films for every feature film they produced in Iran. These changes are likely to have a dramatic negative impact on art cinema films, for they have been shielded from the vagaries of the market by government support.

Fortuitously, a new factor has emerged: the foreign film markets, including those in the Silk Road countries. If managed properly, the income from these markets, which in the late 1990s amounted to several million dollars for certain titles, may be sufficient both to offset government pullback and to protect art cinema films against low public appreciation at home and high competition from abroad.[13] Supported by this newfound source of financing and revenue, several filmmakers, among them Mehrjui, Makhmalbaf (both father and daughter), Panahi, Majidi, Banietemad, and Tahmineh Milani have become relatively independent from both state and private sector financing within Iran. This is a new phenomenon, which, along with the relaxation of restrictions since Khatami's ascendancy, may account for the consolidation of the humanist film genre and the rise of a new political art cinema genre, which have flooded the Iranian and international screens.

HUMANIST AND POLITICAL GENRES   One characteristic of the Iranian art cinema films that has surprised audiences, particularly those outside the country, is its quiet humanism, which stands in sharp contrast to the belligerent rhetoric and the violent politics of the Islamic government. This nontheistic humanism manifests itself in a range of themes and stylistic features. Fatemeh Motamed Aria, a prominent actress, describes this cinema as "compassionate," adding, "It is our plea for compassion that is capturing the world, not our advanced technique or our high technology. Our cinema is being presented to the world because of the kindness of a child toward his sister, or the compassion of a mother towards her child."[14] This concern for others is tied to an optimistic worldview. Accordingly, in this cinema individual efforts for the collective good (often by children) are rewarded, for people are thought to be interdependent, their fate and well-being inextricably bound together.

Surprisingly, for a theocratic state, this cinema is less concerned with the humans' relations with God than with their relation to one another. Also surprisingly, the clerical establishment, individual clergy, and official Islam are generally absent from these films. At the manifest level, the art cinema is intensely personal, social, nontheistic, and unofficial (even anti-official)—forming a quietly counter-hegemonic cinema. But it is not antireligious or anti-Islamic Republic, since it does not oppose the ruling ideology or institutions. There is also a sense that humanistic and ethical values make for a better life here and now as well as in the hereafter (a religious conception).

Some films, even art cinema films, push these ideas to the point of moralism. In Banietemad's *Nargess,* for example, the male protagonist, Adel, is offered a moral choice in the film's last scene, which occurs by the side of a busy freeway. His co-wives represent the two moral positions. One is the pretty, young Nargess who stands for ethical behavior and honesty since she wants Adel to give up thievery; the other is the older, homely Afaq, who wants to continue to live off robbery with Adel. Adel is unable to make the choice; conveniently, fate intervenes in the form of an oncoming truck that runs over Afaq.

If Banietemad followed normative morality in *Nargess,* in her next film, *The May Lady,* she pushed the boundaries of official morality by featuring a divorced single mother documentary filmmaker who insists, despite all odds, on working professionally, raising her teenage son by herself, and maintaining a love relationship with a man to whom she is not married. This is a pivotal film, with its focus on a documentary filmmaker who critically investigates the trauma of women who have lost their children to war, imprisonment, crime, and addiction, and as such bridges the humanist and the political genres.

The best of the art cinema films are imbued with humanist ethics, which means aversion to materialism, a desire for a spiritual center and for decency, and a dogged pursuit of the right path. These, along with the aesthetics of smallness and improvisation, were most emphatically promulgated by Kiarostami. His early film *Where Is the Friend's House?,* described by the Hollywood trade paper *Variety* as "agonizingly slow" but ultimately "rewarding,"[15] was an early key film in this genre. It depicts the relentless efforts of an honest boy to find a friend's house in an adjoining village in order to return the friend's copybook, despite his parent's willful lack of understanding. Such

7.6 *And Life Goes On,* 1992   ethics, dogged optimism, and humanism—tinged with a light touch of irony—became a hallmark of Kiarostami's style, shining through in such films as *And Life Goes On* (*Zindigi Va Digar Hich,* 1992; fig. 7.6) about the aftermath of a massive earthquake in the area in which *Where Is the Friend's House?* was filmed.

However, as Kiarostami evolved into a semiindependent *auteur,* thanks to his maturation, his wide international acclaim, and his revenues from foreign markets, he began to subvert or nuance these humanistic values through self-reflexive and deconstructive narrative strategies. In *Taste of Cherry* (*Tam-i Gilas,* 1997), for example, which centers on a middle-aged man's wish to commit suicide, the director's ironic playfulness casts considerable doubt on the film's narrative outcome (whether the man commits suicide or not) and on Kiarostami's stance toward the moral issues surrounding suicide and the religious edicts against it. In addition, his self-reflexive filming strategies, which highlight the artificiality of film, cast doubt on the certainty of reality, on the clear-cut separation of fact from fiction, and on the authenticity of filmic realism. The production of doubt and ambiguity at so many different levels in a regime that is given to cultural and religious certainty and absolutism is a powerful form of criticism, which is offered, astutely, only at the level of filmic style, not content.

More recently, however, since the ascendancy of Khatami, a type of political art cinema genre has emerged that offers its critique more manifestly at the level of film content. Two examples suffice. Rasul Sadrameli's *Girl in the Sneakers* (*Dokhtari ba kaf-shha-yi katani,* 1999) centers on a budding romance between a young girl and a boy. A family quarrel sends the girl on a "night journey" through the underbelly of Tehran, which forces her to reexamine whether this romance is worth risking alienating her family and facing the dangers that await young single girls in the Islamic Republic. Panahi's *Circle* (*Dayara,* 2000) focuses on the lives of three women prisoners. Two are temporarily released from prison, and the third breaks out of jail to seek an abortion. The dead-end lives of these women as well as those of an addict mother and a prostitute are interwoven with effective realism into a grim tapestry.

In both films, however, the radicalism of the realistic and critical treatment of the women's lives is marred by these male filmmakers' political agenda, which turns their films into conservative narratives with weak female characters and pedantic and forced endings. Both directors offer a rightly critical but unrealistic and pessimistic view of the options women have in society: according to these films, they have none. In *Girl in the Sneakers* the young girl returns home defeated by her night journey, and all the women in *Circle* are sent back to prison. To be sure, there are massive obstacles in the way of women (and men and, for that matter, children) as architects of their own lives in Iran, but this one-dimensional focus on victimization is not only unrealistic and disempowering but also bad filmmaking. Ironically, both films have received high praise internationally, perhaps because they tend to confirm the general view abroad of women in Iran as passive victims of a ruthless patriarchal system.[16]

While the humanist films do not advocate the official religious culture and ideology directly, their emphasis on human-centered worlds, optimism, ethics, and spirituality implicates them in the dominant ideology insofar as these values are similar to the "Islamic values" that the regime regularly professes but only occasionally practices. As a result, the government has tolerated, even welcomed, whatever implicit or explicit criticism these films offer, for they fundamentally oppose neither the ruling doctrine nor the ruling power structure. On the other hand, political films receive official reprimand and censorship. Panahi's *Circle* was banned more than a year, and when the officials of the 2001 Fajr International Film Festival scheduled to screen it, Panahi, in an open letter published in newspapers, refused to allow specialized screenings before the ban on public showing of his film was lifted.[17]

Iranian cinema has come a long way from its localized beginnings in 1900. It has survived and flourished through a complicated multipartner internal dance involving government, private sector, film authors, film industry, and audiences. It has also flourished through the exchange of ideas, products, stories, and genres with the cinemas and societies of both neighboring countries and those in the West. The exigencies of the various hot and cold wars during much of the twentieth century may have limited the range of cinematic exchanges between Iran and the Silk Road countries. However, since the collapse of the Soviet Union, Iranian films have been screened regularly in the Central Asian republics, particularly in Tajikistan, which shares with Iran a long history, Persian language, Iranian culture and arts, and Islam. In the 1990s this exchange intensified when Mohsen Makhmalbaf filmed his poetic *Silence* (*Sukut,* 1998) there, showcasing the arts, crafts, music, language, and culture of Tajikistan even though in an exoticized fashion. The film is banned in Iran, however, stopping the flow of cinematic and cultural exchange between the two countries that it had promised.

The high quality of art cinema films and the wide international success they now enjoy may be temporary, however, for the solution to the multifaceted challenges ahead require that the government and film industry muster sufficient foresight, political will, social stability, and economic growth to sustain the industry long enough so that it can become self-sufficient. Recent events suggest that political will and social stability, like economic health, are fragile commodities in Iran. •

This essay is a considerably revised version of "Iranian Cinema," which appeared in *Life and Art: The New Iranian Cinema,* ed. Rose Issa and Sheila Whitaker (London: National Film Theatre, 1999), pp. 43–65. It is published here with permission. All images courtesy of the Farabi Cinema Foundation, Tehran, Iran.

1   Hamid Naficy, "Iranian Feature Films: A Brief Critical History," *Quarterly Review Film Studies* 4 (1979): 450.

2   Mohammad Ali Issari, *Cinema in Iran, 1900–1979* (Metuchen, N.J.: Scarecrow Press, 1989), pp. 164–94. See also Hamid Naficy, *Iran Media Index* (Westport, Conn.: Greenwood Press, 1984), pp. 190–220.

3   Naficy, "Iranian Feature Films," p. 451.

4   "Persian Filmmakers Map Expansion into International Market; Eye Co-productions," *Variety,* November 12, 1969.

5   Hamid Naficy, "Islamizing Film Culture in Iran," in *Iran: Political Culture in the Islamic Republic,* ed. Samih K. Farsoun and Mehrdad Mashayekhi (London: Routledge, 1992), pp. 182–83.

6   Ibid., pp. 184–87.

7   For theorization and description of this culture, see Hamid Naficy, *The Making of Exile Cultures: Iranian Television in Los Angeles* (Minneapolis: University of Minnesota Press, 1993).

8   Hamid Naficy, *An Accented Cinema: Exilic and Diasporic Filmmaking* (Princeton, N.J.: Princeton University Press, 2001).

9   For these regulations, see Naficy, "Islamizing Film Culture in Iran," pp. 190–92.

10 Hamid Naficy, "Veiled Voice and Vision in Iranian Cinema: The Evolution of Rakhshan Banietemad's Films," in *Ladies and Gentlemen, Boys and Girls: Gender in Film at the End of the 20th Century,* ed. Murray Pomerance (New York: State University of New York Press, 2001).

11 *Mahnameh-ye Sinemai-ye Film* 135 (20 Dey 1371/January 1993), p. 8.

12 *Mahnameh-ye Sinemai-ye Film* 134 (Dey 1371/December 1992), p. 19.

13 For example, Majid Majidi's Oscar-nominated *Children of Heaven* (*Bachihha-yi Asiman,* 1997) earned more than $1 million in four months in ten Hong Kong cinemas alone, taking a position among the top-ten box-office earners of the summer. It also grossed another $1 million in its limited release in the United States.

14 Quoted in "Jashn-i Cinema Avay-i Mihrabani-yi Mast," *Hamshahri,* September 15, 1999 at www.neda.net/hamshahri/780624/adabh.htm.

15 *Variety,* August 16, 1989.

16 *Circle,* for example, won the Golden Lion for the best film at the Venice International Film Festival and was sold, according to its distributor, for commercial distribution to an unprecedented twenty-nine countries. See "*Dayara* dar 29 keshvar-e jahan bi namayish darmiaiad," *Hamshahri,* December 14, 2000, at www.iranian.com/News/2000/December/circle.html.

17 "Jafar Panahi: Az namayish-c Dayara khoddari mikonam," *Dowran-e Emruz,* January 9, 2001, at www.iranian.com/News/2001/January/circle.html.

The Ancient Art in Xinjiang, China. Urumqi: Xinjiang Art and Photography Press, 1994.

A picture book of major artistic discoveries.

Barber, E. J. W. *Prehistoric Textiles.* Princeton, N.J.: Princeton University Press, 1991; and *Women's Work: The First 20,000 Years.* New York: W. W. Norton, 1994.

Studies of the origin and development of spinning and weaving in early western Eurasia (Iran to Britain), the former detailing the technical history and the latter the social and economic history.

————. *The Mummies of Ürümchi.* New York: W. W. Norton; London: Macmillan, 1999.

Description of the oldest mummies found in Xinjiang and their splendidly preserved clothing, with hypotheses about their origins and life-styles, based principally on textile, ecological, and linguistic connections.

Basilov, Vladimir N. "The Scythian Harp and the Kazakh Kobyz: In Search of Historical Connections." In *Foundations of Empire,* edited by Gary Seaman, pp. 77–100. Los Angeles: Ethnographic Press, University of Southern California, 1992.

A careful reconstructive analysis of the earliest preserved bowed instrument.

Brend, Barbara. *Islamic Art.* Cambridge, Mass.: Harvard University Press, 1991.

Traces the development of Islamic art from the seventh through the twentieth century.

Fisher, Robert E. *Buddhist Art and Architecture.* London: Thames and Hudson, 1993.

Accessible introduction to pan-Asian Buddhist art and architecture.

Franck, Irene M., and David M. Brownstone. *The Silk Road: A History.* New York and Oxford: Facts on File Publications, 1986.

Popular history of the Silk Road, emphasizing travelers through the ages.

Hayashi, Ryoichi. *The Silk Road and the Shoso-in,* translated by Robert Ricketts. New York: Weatherhill, 1975.

Discussion of the Silk Road from a Japanese perspective, focusing on the extraordinary group of eighth-century, Silk Road–related objects in the Shosoin Collection in Nara, Japan.

Issa, Rose, and Sheila Whitaker, eds. *Life and Art: The New Iranian Cinema.* London: National Film Theatre, 1999.

An anthology of scholarly articles on the Iranian post-revolutionary cinema, including two by Hamid Naficy.

Issari, Mohammad Ali. *Cinema in Iran, 1900–1979.* Metuchen, N.J.: Scarecrow Press, 1989.

A history of the Iranian cinema from the beginning to the revolution of 1978–79, with an emphasis on documentaries and United States Information Agency films made and distributed in Iran.

Izu, Kenro. *Light over Ancient Angkor: Platinum Prints.* New York: Friends Without A Border, 1996.

Contains statements by the artist as well as his photographs of Angkor.

Juliano, Annette L., and Judith A. Lerner. *Monks and Merchants: Silk Road Treasures from Northwest China, Gansu and Ningxia, 4th–7th century.* New York: Harry N. Abrams, Inc., and Asia Society, Inc., 2001.

Recent and highly informative catalogue of artworks from northwest China.

Klimburg-Salter, Deborah E. *The Kingdom of Bamiyan: The Buddhist Art and Culture of the Hindu Kush.* Naples and Rome: Istituto Universitario Orientale & Ismeo, 1989.

Monograph on the Buddhist site of Bamiyan, whose colossal Buddhas were destroyed in 2001.

———. *The Silk Route and the Diamond Path: Esoteric Buddhist Art on the Trans-Himalayan Trade Routes.* Los Angeles: UCLA Art Council, 1982.

Catalogue of artworks from the trans-Himalayan region with useful essays on the religion, history, and geography of the area.

Levin, Theodore. *The Hundred Thousand Fools of God: Musical Travels in Central Asia (and Queens, New York).* Bloomington and Indianapolis: Indiana University Press, 1996.

Discusses the cultural and political history of Central Asia in tsarist, Soviet, and post-Soviet times through encounters with musicians in Uzbekistan, Tajikistan, and Queens, New York (émigré Bukharan Jews).

Linduff, Katheryn M., Han Rubin, and Sun Shuyun, eds. *The Beginnings of Metallurgy in China.* Lewiston, Queenston: Edwin Mellen Press, 2000.

Compilation of recent scholarly findings on early metallurgy in China.

Mallory, James, and Victor H. Mair. *The Tarim Mummies.* London: Thames and Hudson, 2000.

Broad survey of the Xinjiang mummies down to historic times, with hypotheses about their origins based on genetic, linguistic, and general archaeological evidence.

Mannikka, Eleanor. *Angkor Wat: Time, Space, and Kinship.* Honolulu: University of Hawai'i Press, 1996.

Discusses the art and architecture of the twelfth-century temple complex of Angkor Wat in Cambodia, relating its layout and physical dimensions to calendrical calculations.

Needham, Joseph. "The Evolution of Iron and Steel Technology in East and Southeast Asia." In *The Coming of the Age of Iron.* pp. 507–39. New Haven and London: Yale University Press, 1980.

Summary of a leading scholar's viewpoint on the diffusion of iron technology to China and the indigenous development of cast iron.

Rudenko, Sergei I. *Frozen Tombs of Siberia,* translated by M. W. Thompson. Berkeley: University of California Press, 1970.

Description of the spectacular finds from Scythian tombs of the fourth through third century B.C.E. frozen by permafrost in the Altai Mountains.

Sass, Stephen L. *The Substance of Civilization.* New York: Arcade Publishing, 1998.

Discussion of the development of materials and their importance to civilization, from the viewpoint of a materials scientist (largely oriented to West Asia and Europe).

Schafer, Edward H. *The Golden Peaches of Samarkand: A Study of T'ang Exotics.* Berkeley: University of California Press, 1963.

Fascinating compendium of the tremendous variety of objects, customs, and ideas that the Chinese imported via the Silk Road during the Tang dynasty (618–907).

Sheng, Bright. "The Love Songs of Qinghai." *Asian Art & Culture: Music* 8, no. 3 (Fall 1995): 51–67.

Illustrated exploration of music of Qinghai Province.

ten Grotenhuis, Elizabeth. *Japanese Mandalas: Representations of Sacred Geography.* Honolulu: University of Hawai'i Press, 1999.

Introduction to Japanese mandalas (representations of realms of enlightenment), discussing the appropriation and transformation of Indian and Chinese models.

Vollmer, John E., et al. *Silk Roads, China Ships: An Exhibition of East-West Trade.* Toronto: Royal Ontario Museum, 1983.

Catalogue of artworks representative of east-west trade on both overland and sea routes.

Whitfield, Susan. *Life Along the Silk Road.* Berkeley and Los Angeles: University of California Press, 1999.

Engaging reconstruction of the eastern Silk Road during the eighth through the tenth century as seen through the lives of ten composite characters.

INDEX